# THE BIBLE IN PASTORAL CARE

*Books by*
WAYNE E. OATES
*Published by The Westminster Press*

The Bible in Pastoral Care
The Christian Pastor

# *The Bible in Pastoral Care*

## WAYNE E. OATES

*Philadelphia*

THE WESTMINSTER PRESS

Library of Congress Catalogue Card Number: 52-11246

PRINTED IN THE UNITED STATES OF AMERICA

*To*
GAINES S. DOBBINS

## CONTENTS

# PREFACE

THE average pastor longs for specific guidance as to how the Bible may best be used in a healing way to bring insight and restoration of soul to the individual persons with whom he counsels. In his theological courses, he usually receives extensive training in the historical study of the Scripture. He gains access to the wealth of critical scholarship, wrought out by devout scholars who suffered privation, ridicule, and bodily danger that we might have a perfected and scientifically validated text. The Bible has successfully stood tests of literary and historical validation more crucial than those applied to any other group of documents. The pastor is encompassed about by a great " cloud of witnesses," therefore, when he begins to use his Bible creatively and redemptively even as he himself also is an instrument of the Holy Spirit.

Likewise, the pastor receives extensive training in the use of the Bible in preaching and public worship, as well as religious education. His use of the Bible at these points, however, often leads him into particularly difficult pastoral care situations. One of the purposes of this volume is to give attention to some of these problems.

It is just at these points that a minimum of training is given the pastor as to the distinctly *pastoral use of the Bible*. He encounters parishioners' questions, conflicts, doubts, and fears.

Here he is thrown back on the unexamined and naïve methods which he has learned by chance in the community folklore upon which he " cut his religious teeth." A curious combination of warmth and tenderness and almost cruel malpractice is quite often the result. It is the task of teachers in the field of pastoral care to lay hold of the unsystematized mass of community wisdom and organize that warmth and tenderness in such a way that it can be taught to ministers and particularly to students in theological schools. On the other hand, it is the task of teachers in pastoral care also to bring psychological knowledge and ethical insight to bear upon the malpractice of using the Bible in such a way that people are further confused by the instrument that God intended for their help.

The indiscriminate and often harmful ways in which the Bible has been used by many ministers have caused many well-trained pastors to avoid the use of the Bible in their face-to-face ministries to individuals. Nevertheless, the minister has long enough been confronted with two equally unsatisfactory alternatives. He has had to choose between either using the proof-text application of a few narrowly circumscribed verses to " sell " mechanical patterns of salvation to people or, on the other hand, leaving the Bible entirely out of his personal counseling of individuals in favor of mechanical theories of personality and counseling proposed by modern psychotherapists. Surely there is some other more excellent way of implementing our precious spiritual heritage without falling prey to the evils of the worship of the letter, and at the same time without losing the substantial gains made by a careful psychology of counseling.

Clinically trained ministers have quite often had valuable experience in dealing with acutely sick patients in hospitals but comparatively little training in the pastoral care of relatively healthy and productive persons whom they meet in the average pastoral situation. Naturally, with acutely psychotic persons the Bible, like every other resource, should be used only by a minister skilled in understanding the distorted religious consciousness of these patients. Nevertheless, the average minister is in a different social situation ordinarily, although he does occasionally deal with acutely disturbed persons and can learn much from them about the use of religious guidance in *preventing* emotional disorders.

Then, too, many ministers, trained in the modern techniques of counseling, have been influenced greatly by what is known as "nondirective" techniques of counseling. Such ministers face the dilemma of using what they have validated as sound counseling procedures, and at the same time meeting the real needs of their people for help on their use of the Bible. Person-centered counseling insights have much to offer in developing a health-giving attitude in the pastoral use of the Bible. What is said here concerning the use of the Bible is said with full knowledge of the valuable work that competent research persons have done in the field of counseling, as well as with full knowledge of the exceeding greatness of the authoritarian atmosphere that the Bible lends to the relationship of a pastor to an individual. I am acutely aware of the way in which a minister can hide his own "blind spots" and spiritual inadequacies under a Biblical quotation. Nevertheless, the pastor who uses the Bible as a means of interpretation, comfort, and prayer in his individual pastoral ministry cannot be dominated by the concepts of men and women who are functioning in a secular environment, and who do not accept any responsibility for the religious life of the persons with whom they work.

People still come to pastors for specific guidance, comfort, and prayer, all of which are made possible through the use of the Bible. If the pastor does not function fully and effectively at this point, this ministry either goes unperformed or is taken over by superstitious and ignorant people who have had no disciplined study of the Bible, but who, nevertheless, take the Bible seriously as to its place in life. Therefore, the contents of this volume have been written with the objective of giving specific, detailed, and positive suggestions to the average pastor as to the use of the Bible in pastoral care and personal counseling.

## ACKNOWLEDGMENTS

I am indebted to Dr. Russell L. Dicks, Dr. Simon Doniger, and Dr. Paul Meacham for invaluable editorial guidance on this manuscript. Their depth and breadth of vision, their careful personal attention, and their profound encouragement and acceptance have taught me much about the arts and crafts of writing, and even more about the meaning of the Christian fellowship.

Likewise, I am indebted to the president and trustees of the Southern Baptist Theological Seminary, who arranged a brief leave of absence from my duties as a teacher, part of which I spent in writing these pages. I am deeply grateful also to Professor G. S. Dobbins, my senior colleague, and to Chaplain Joseph Knowles and Rev. Eugene Mandrell, all of whom carried on my teaching in my absence.

Furthermore, I am grateful to the faculty and students at Union Theological Seminary in New York for the fellowship of learning and the provision of a " home away from home " at which I could work creatively. Particularly am I indebted to the members of the Department of Religious Education with whom I studied and taught as I, with their comradeship, formulated the thoughts in this book.

The religious heritage which I have received, one in which the Bible is considered intensely relevant for all of life, given to me by my grandmother first, then by my mother, and clarified for me at the hands of my college and university professors, is due a real debt of appreciation from me. This is a debt that cannot be repaid, but only continually appropriated in my pastoral ministry.

My wife has read and reread the manuscript in order that my meaning shall be clear and unencumbered with jargon. My son, Bill, has been to me a happy companion on long walks, and real fun when life becomes too serious.

Miss Dorothy Hollis has typed and retyped the manuscript from my illegible longhand, and has my profound appreciation.

WAYNE E. OATES.

*New York City,*
*April, 1952*

## Chapter I

# THE SYMBOLIC USE OF THE BIBLE

THE Bible has an overwhelming symbolic strength. The fact that a statement is in the Bible endows that statement with a peculiar power, for weal or for woe. To the person who lives next to nature, who is relatively unsophisticated, and who has not developed a critical world view, the Bible is even as the Ark of the Covenant: to lay unconsecrated hands upon it is to die. This symbolic significance of the Bible lives on also in the more primitive consciousness of apparently sophisticated people, who express their uneasiness by never talking about it, by allowing it to remain in the realm of the mysterious to them, or by compulsively rejecting its wisdom with an undifferentiated prejudice.

The Bible as a symbol has many uses in the counseling ministry of a pastor. He may use it as a means of identifying himself as a minister of religion to those with whom he counsels. A copy of the Bible in full sight on the minister's desk immediately identifies him as a Christian to the person who comes to his study for counsel. It has always been fascinating to me to observe a person who comes to my office as his gaze shifts half-consciously to the bookshelves, to the objects on my desk. The pictures of my family identify me as a husband and a father, the picture of Jesus and the rich young ruler identifies me as a friend of Jesus, and the Bible identifies me as one who may be able to deal with some of his questions about it. All these symbols do much to clarify my relationships in life to the person who seeks my help, thereby relieving me of the necessity of too much explanatory conversation.

The nonliturgical Protestant minister, who wears no special clerical garb, quite regularly finds himself at a loss as to how to identify himself to strangers when he visits them. But the stranger who sits down beside someone on a train, bus, or plane who is reading the Bible usually presumes that he is sitting by a minister. The relatively uniform appearance of most Bibles has given a clarity to its symbolism. So often is this true that the minister who is not particularly eager to appear as a "holier than thou" person as he travels is grateful for the publication of Bibles in bindings like other books. Nevertheless, the stranger who sees the black leather-bound, India-paper volume knows in a deep way to whom he is speaking and who speaks to him.

The Bible can be used as a symbol to great advantage in certain difficult pastoral care situations. Examples from my own ministry are illustrative.

I was called to a local hospital at the request of a woman whom I did not know at all. The woman, according to the nurse, was deaf and was at the point of death. She wanted a minister in her last hour. I happen to belong to a denomination in which the ministers wear no distinguishing symbols of clothing. The woman could not distinguish me from a doctor, and I was not able to tell her verbally who I was because she was deaf. In order to communicate with her, I reached into my pocket and produced a small, black, gilt-edged Bible. I held it before her and began to read. She smiled a light of recognition. I prayed, folding my hands in reverence, hoping she could read lips. She faintly smiled her gratitude.

Another person whom I served as pastor over the tedious months of a chronic illness lived in a humble rural home. She had served her church and her family well, and had leaned heavily upon the Bible. As her pastor, I knew the quiet symbolism of the shift of her gaze as she began to tire of conversation. She would turn her face away from me to a spot behind a little radio on her bedside table. There was a worn and much-read Bible. Her shifted gaze always told me in a tacit understanding that she wanted me to read to her. This was an unspoken liturgy of the spirit re-enacted at each visit. The Bible to her was a symbol of an understood fellowship of prayer in suffering.

However, honest attention must be given here to the misuse of the Bible as a symbol. It may become little more than a fetish with which to cajole the demons that possess the spirits of men. As such it may become an instrument of the demonic, and the devil will begin to cite Scripture for his own purposes.

For instance, a thirty-two-year-old man was plagued by homosexual thoughts, and caught in the grip of homosexual habits. He went to his pastor with his problem, in order to get guidance, relief, and hope. His pastor gave him strong advice about how to control himself, and gave him a copy of the Bible to read in the midst of his temptations. He said, " When you go to bed at night, place this Bible under your pillow, and it will drive away your evil thoughts and dreams and help you to rest." The man was at the time on the verge of a paranoid mental breakdown, and a few more days of faithful adherence to his pastor's guidance hastened his hospitalization. The point at which I interviewed the patient was in the receiving ward of a State hospital of which I was chaplain at the time. He felt at that time that God had given him up to " a reprobate mind," and that he should die. Here the Bible was used as a fetish, sincerely intended to heal; actually, however, it became a tool of the self-destructive processes already in motion in his life.

Such an example of the unwitting malpractice of ministers clearly illustrates two important clinical pastoral observations which need to be noted here. First, the pastor who carefully observes the *effects* of his use of the Bible in pastoral care situations soon begins to feel the heavy pull of authoritarianism added to his relationship by his use of it. If he is as concerned as he should be about maintaining a " permissive " relationship of relaxation, free of threat, he finds that the Bible often reduces permissiveness, creates tension, and introduces elements of threat into his pastoral context.

Why is this? It is because the Bible is nothing but a symbol of authority to many people. Culturally, the Bible is a transversal symbol of authority in the social structure of Protestantism and in the religious consciousness of Protestants. It is the minister's task to see to it that in his community the Bible is not just a symbol of authority, but that it has actual meaning as well. As a symbol of authority, the Bible is both a sword and a shield for the pastor. It becomes easily an instrument whereby the minister expresses his hostility and a means of protection when he feels threatened. When the minister finds himself in an environment in which the Bible is not an agreed-upon symbol of culture and authority, as is true in a large university or on a mission field, he discovers the necessity of translating the Bible out of the realm of the authoritarian and the symbolic and into the realm of the interpreted meaningfulness and the interpersonal realities which are understandable by those with whom he deals and whose suffering he seeks to relieve. It was just such a ministry that Jesus rendered when he reinterpreted the Scriptures so that they gave life rather than destroyed it. The lament that Isaiah felt in his day becomes a challenge to the modern minister: " All vision is become unto you as the words of a book that is sealed, which men deliver to one that is learned, saying, Read this, I pray thee; and he saith, I cannot, for it is sealed: and the book is delivered to him that is not learned, saying, Read this, I pray thee; and he saith, I am not learned " (Isa. 29:11, 12).

This points to the second clinical pastoral observation, i.e., much of the damage done by ministers in their misuse of the Bible is caused by their own undisciplined dependence upon its symbolic use rather than their careful use of it as a teaching come from God. That was the weakness of the pastor's methodology in telling the man to trust in the Bible by putting it under his pillow. The healing power of Scriptural truth lies in its appropriation by means of a deepened insight and quickened understanding, not by the fearful use of the book itself as a symbol for worship. The Bible may be misused even as the symbol of the cross, which is too often taken as a trinket to hang around the neck. Both may be little more than good-luck charms. Such a use of the cross is vastly different from being able to say, " I have been crucified with Christ."

Also, the absence of ritual among nonliturgical Protestants has resulted in their ritualistic use of " daily Bible-reading," without investing it with meaning, direction, and purpose. This feeds the obsessional trends within a personality, and great care should be used when urging people in groups to read their Bibles daily. Care should be used to follow up these exhortations with specific ways in which the Bible may be used, and by giving as much personal supervision to the reading as possible. Small group discussions should be developed in such a way that the reading becomes a means of meeting specific personal needs, and not merely an end within itself whereby the patient atones for his guilt, allays his anxieties, and appeases the wrath of the pastor.

Examples of the misuse of the Bible as a symbol cause many persons, particularly psychologists and psychiatrists, to react negatively and to avoid its every appearance in the thought life of troubled people. Some pastors might feel that the use of the Bible with people who are hostile toward religion drives them farther from it still, and that the use of the Bible with fanatically religious persons increases their blindness.

My own answer to this is that these hostilities and prejudices need to be evaluated in the beginning, and that it is better for the person to know from the beginning that he is talking to a minister if the relationship is to move honestly and smoothly. If the person feels hostile, it is better that the pastor know it as early as possible. But more than that, I feel that many people with whom we deal are so uninformed religiously that they will have little or no feeling about a Bible as a symbol. They will prefer that the pastor minister to them on a purely " horizontal " or human level. A minister needs to identify himself from the beginning by defining his relationship, to say the least, by the presence of one of the agreed-upon symbols of Protestant Christianity — the Bible — on his desk, in his waiting room, and in his living room at home.

But the main reason for such a contention is that the majority of the people to whom the pastor ministers are persons for whom the Bible has a positive, healthy, and precious meaning. It represents comfort and strength in the presence of life's typical crises — birth, baptism, marriage, parenthood, disappointment, pain, and death. They see it as a source of light and truth, as the one thing most dependable in the welter and confusion of all that they see and hear. It symbolizes security and understanding, truth and love. It symbolizes judgment for the things that they know to be wrong by any standard of wisdom they themselves would choose. Therefore, they respond to the symbol and the teacher who accompanies it as an ethically well-balanced friend responds to an ethically well-balanced friend.

The pastor who is honest with himself, however, knows that

some of the people who do feel deeply affectionate toward the Bible and its profound communications nevertheless present to him a distorted religious consciousness. Their use of the Bible is in keeping with the pathology of their personalities. The mentally sick person often expresses his problem in age-old symbols, and the symbols of the Bible become means whereby he desperately attempts to communicate his distress to a world of "average" conformists to a superficial reality with which he is losing, or has lost, touch. It is as if he were on an Isle of Patmos, fearful of speaking plainly lest his captors destroy him; therefore, he phrases his revelations of the inner world in symbols that appear as nonsense to the outer world of threatening dictatorships. He depends upon the minister as an interpreter to discern his meaning.

Thus the symbols of the Bible become the language of the spirit between the acutely disturbed patient and the minister as the minister goes "underground" into the labyrinthine catacombs of the inner world with a mental patient who is religiously conscious and states his problem in the symbols of the Bible. (The rest of this chapter is embodied in my article "The Diagnostic Use of the Bible," *Pastoral Psychology*, December, 1950.)

The Bible is the pastor's "royal road" to the deeper levels of the personalities of his people, and particularly to those who are deeply disturbed. Traditionally the Bible has been used by ministers as a means of reassurance and comfort to people whom they visit and who come to them for counseling help. More recently, Bonnell and Dicks have stimulated a fresh appreciation of the Bible as devotional literature in pastoral care and as an instrument of religious discipline.

The use of the Bible as an instrument of diagnosis, however, needs initial attention and extended study. The question needs to be asked, "Does the Biblical material in the stream of speech of an emotionally disturbed person give a pastor a ' royal road ' toward understanding something of the dynamic causes of the person's distress? "

Oskar Pfister, in his book *Christianity and Fear,* gives a positive, generalized answer when he says, " Tell me what you find in the Bible, and I will tell you what you are." Here the Bible is seen, not only as a record of the revelation of God to men, but as an instrument of the revelation of the personality of both the minister and the person with whom he counsels.

This concept is suggested by at least one passage in the Bible itself. In James 1:22–24, the writer says: " Be doers of the word, and not hearers only, deceiving yourselves. For if any one is a hearer of the word and not a doer, he is like a man who observes his natural face in a mirror; for he observes himself and goes away and at once forgets what he was like." The implication is that the Bible is a mirror into which a person projects his own concept of himself, and which in turn reflects it back with accuracy.

The Bible, then, is to the Protestant pastor as dream symbolism and superego functions are to the psychoanalyst. The meaningful symbols and ethical realities of the Bible have dynamic connections with the forces at work in the less accessible areas of the personality of the counselee. As a fast-moving epic of human history, the Bible story itself is a psychodrama of abiding fidelity to the functional laws of personality. Likewise, the Bible as a book of pictorial illustration is to the pastor what the thematic apperception test is to the clinical psychologist. As Gardner Murphy describes this test, it is based upon the principle that the individual has specific needs that occur in response to the " press " of the environmental situation. A unified expression and need are perceived out of the individual's total background of experience and projected upon art forms in a mirrorlike fashion. The objective of the test is to get " a wide diversity of individual interpretations given " (*Personality: A Biosocial Approach to Origins and Structure,* p. 671. Harper & Brothers, 1947).

Applying this principle and objective to his use of the Bible as a means of insight into the deeper problems of people, the pastor himself is reminded of the fact that the main frustration he has faced in the use of the Bible has been that among Protestants there is such a " wide diversity of interpretations given." These interpretations may be of very little value as accurate objective exegeses of the Scripture, but they are of intrinsic subjective value as reflections of what manner of person the individual is who gives the interpretations. In a word, the interpretation reflects more concerning the inter- preter and his life situation than it does of the Bible itself.

Especially is this true in the case of acutely disturbed per- sons. The more secure and mature a person is, the more capable he is of discerning and interpreting accurately the meaning and content of the Bible. The less secure and more immature a person is, the more likely he will be to quote Scripture for his own purposes. In these latter cases, the pastor (granted that he himself is secure, mature, and informed in his own relation to the Bible and also to the psychodynamics of personality) can get a fairly clear-cut understanding of the life situation of the person with whom he is counseling as well as a feeling for the purposive drift of his life energies.

Three clinical examples of these facts demonstrate best the diagnostic use of the Bible.

Mrs. M. H. is a 24-year-old woman, married, having no chil- dren. She came to her pastor's attention when she complained of having committed the unpardonable sin, which she interpreted as " cursing God." She felt that she had called God a g— d— s. o. b., and that there was no forgiveness.

Later, she was admitted to a general hospital as the patient of a private psychiatrist. The psychiatrist interpreted her problem to the pastor as arising from " feelings of inadequacy in her estimate of herself as a woman, as a sexual partner, and as a social being." He diagnosed her as a severe obsessional neurotic with schizoid tendencies. The recurrent obsessive " cursing thoughts " and self-derogatory attitudes were interpreted as a sort of mental hypochondriasis.

The patient was preoccupied with Scripture verses and constantly demanded interpretations of the following passages in the New Testament: " These Scripture verses keep worrying me, and I cannot figure my way out: ' If you repent and then continue in sin, there is no way to repent again without crucifying Christ afresh ' " (a paraphrase of Heb. 6:4–6, and 10:26, 27). On the second interview, she said: " I think of myself as the wicked servant in the parable of the Talents. I have taken my gifts and buried them, and I have a master who is too hard for me. I want to submit myself to him, but I just can't seem to do so fully." On the fourth interview, she repeated this parable and gave an added interpretation: " I just don't seem to be able to use myself like I want to — it's myself — I just can't seem to do so."

On a fifth interview, she asked this question: " What does that Scripture mean when it says that men and women should not be married who are unequally yoked together? " (compare this paraphrase wth II Cor. 6:14, I Cor. 6:6, and Deut. 22:10 for the disparity between the historical record and the projected effect).

The history detail shows that this woman was a Presbyterian before her marriage. After marriage she joined the Baptist church in her community in response to pressure from her husband and her mother-in-law. The girl felt guilty about having married and moved away from her mother, who had been a mental patient in a State hospital. She also felt quite inferior to her mother-in-law and incapable of " winning her husband's affections " away from his mother. In the intimacy of sexual relations she was frigid, and could not " use herself as she would like."

The unequalness of the life situation was accurate, and it is very probable that the apostle Paul was specifically referring to the institution of marriage. Likewise, the " buried gifts " in this instance could indicate something of the sense of ethical necessity the woman had about being an adequate marital partner. However, the master in the drama undoubtedly was the husband who had usurped the place of God in the woman's life. The idolatry of the " master " ended in desecration — the god in the case was an s. o. b.! And the reference to idols in II Cor., ch. 6, was entirely appropriate to her.

Miss S. R., a 43-year-old woman, single, high school education. Patient in a State hospital. Upon admission showed general loss of interest in things about her except in that she was compelled to visit all the neighbors excessively, with no apparent reason at all and at inappropriate times. Obsessed with the idea that something was " about to happen to her sister."

In the first interview with this patient, the chaplain learned that her father had been a lay preacher and that her father had " petted her a lot." This included taking her on his lap, sleeping with her until she was " fourteen and after." The father brought another minister to " board at the home." She and the sister mentioned above both fell in love with this man, who was an older person whose first wife had died. A keen rivalry developed, and the patient's sister finally succeeded in marrying the man. The patient then went to live with the sister and her husband. The marriage between the minister and the patient's sister ended in divorce at the time of the hospitalization of the patient.

Not only did the sister defeat the patient in the case of the marriage, but also the patient felt that the sister was the favorite of the mother, and that some of the family money had been used to send her to college, whereas the patient did not get to go.

This history information is exceptionally significant in light of the use that the patient made of her Bible. Being a very religiously inclined person, she laid great store by her Bible. She referred repeatedly to the fact that she loved the story of Jacob, Rachel, and Leah better than any other part of the Bible. She was asked to tell the story. The patient said: " Leah married Jacob before Rachel did, but he and Rachel were finally married anyway and it turned out right."

The sibling rivalry situation of this patient was integrally related to the affective value attached to the Biblical story. The psychodramatic situation was re-enacted in the interpretation.

" The third patient is a 25-year-old woman, married, the mother of a five-year-old daughter. She is well oriented to time, place, and situation. She is noticeably tense and a little shy. She has an eighth grade education, belongs to a Baptist church.

" She came to the hospital because of an attempt to take the life of her child. She had entered the room while the child was sleeping, took a pair of scissors, and was standing over the child to kill her when the husband came into the room and stopped the proceedings. The patient explained that she felt called of the Lord to sacrifice the child after having heard a sermon the same evening on Abraham's sacrifice of Isaac. The minister had greatly dramatized the story.

" She expressed the fear that she had perhaps committed the unpardonable sin (not necessarily in connection with the child). The child had been begotten out of wedlock; the father had to be brought home from the Army for the wedding at a rather late stage of the pregnancy. The patient was living with her parents and was the decided favorite of her father. But the father was not willing to forgive her. He sent her out of the home telling her that she was not ' fit to live with the other children.' She has not yet found her way back into the affection of the father. She lived with an aunt until the husband returned from overseas two years after the marriage.

" The husband had selected the child as the center of his affection, leaving the patient greatly isolated. He did things for the child, forgetting his wife on almost every occasion. He seemed to have no respect or love for her.

" The woman frequently says she cannot understand her own behavior since she insists, weeping, that she loves the child. She comes gradually, however, to see that she has some unbridled aggression toward the child. This aggression seems to revolve about the fact that the child has actually been the causal agent in separating her from her father's affection and from that of her husband.

" The sermon on Abraham served as a precipitating point in the attempt to discharge her aggression under the guise of a sacrifice to God. Indications are that the earthly father is the god in this case, and the child becomes a sacrifice or peace offering. The patient appears to be attempting to remove the cause of the original isolation in getting rid of the child. She is out of fellowship with her god, the father, and it is of such long duration that she wonders if the unpardonable sin against him has not been committed.

" The patient gradually comes to see who her god is, and takes responsibility for her aggression toward the child. She is able to make a fairly good adjustment at home " (Madden, Myron C., " The Contribution of Søren Kierkegaard to a Christian Psychology." Unpublished thesis, Southern Baptist Theological Seminary, 1950).

In no sense are these cases quoted in a " proof-text " way. They are illustrative, however, of the integral relationship between the dynamic causes of the patients' illness and the use that they make of Biblical material. These persons are acutely disturbed, and a bold connection is easily seen between their problems and their effective grasp of Biblical material. Less disturbed persons would not react so obviously.

Furthermore, it is plainly evident that to argue with these patients over their interpretations would only serve to seal off insight and lucid religious thinking, rather than to convince them. Again, it is obvious that the patients herein described were persons who attached great feeling to religion as such. They were not like the vast majority of people in a secular culture — Biblical illiterates.

This creates the need for a further exploration of the use of the Bible in re-education of a disturbed person. Furthermore, the diagnostic and therapeutic uses of the Bible involve equal danger as they promise help in pastoral counseling. But this is no justification for ignoring the Bible, or taking it away from the patients or depreciating the importance of its ideas to them.

Rather, the minister necessarily must know in comprehensiveness and detail the dramatic story, the literary structure, the historical context, the principles of exegesis, and the psychology of the Bible. Likewise, he needs the benefit of disciplined experience in a clinical counseling relationship with large numbers of people who seek his help. He must be acquainted with " living human documents " as well as ancient manuscripts.

## CHAPTER II

## LEGALISM AND THE USE OF THE BIBLE

THE use of the Bible in the teaching functions of the Christian community naturally makes of it a book of personal and corporate discipline. One of the great purposes for the original writing of many portions of the Bible, especially of the New Testament, was to throw ethical and spiritual light upon the practical ethical dilemmas with which the spiritual community collided. This makes the book relevant to those same practical concerns of Christians today, even though the social and historical context in which we face these problems is quite different from that of first century Christians. Therefore, the Bible, in the hands of contemporary Christians, is a handbook of church and personal discipline, a treasury of ideals of human thought, feeling, and conduct as these experiences are lived out under the rule of God. Thus, the participation of the authors of the Bible in the eternity of the new being in Christ, as well as the weathering tests of history, makes of the Bible a book that speaks with an independent reality.

Nevertheless, the basic question we confront here is, How shall the Bible be used in the application of these ideals to specific human situations today? The minister bears the necessary tensions between being a preacher of the ideals of Jesus, on the one hand, and manifesting the pastoral tenderness of Jesus toward persons who have failed to measure up to those ideals, on the other hand. K. E. Kirk, in his book *The Vision of God,* says that the pastor has two alternatives: to use the teachings of the Bible and the Church *pastorally* or to use them *penally*. By the pastoral use of the Bible, he would mean "such uses . . . as are designed to comfort, strengthen, and inspire the weakling." By the penal use of the Bible and its ideals, he would mean "such usages as have for their purpose to cut off the Church from the world by cutting the weakling from the Church" (*The Vision of God,* p. 467. Longmans, Green & Co., Inc., 1934).

The use of the Bible as a treasury of ideals may very easily be twisted into its legalistic use as a book of penal discipline by means of which the pastor introduces Biblical authority as legal justification for his own merciless judgment of human frailty. Having rejected this role as "one who excommunicates," however, the minister still faces his responsibility as a protector of the flock from those external forces that would destroy the community itself. Naturally, I am aware that I am presupposing the whole problem of the nature and intention of the Bible, and the role of the minister in his relation to the Bible and to his people, when I raise this issue.

The pastor who uses the Bible as a lawbook casts himself into the role of a legalistic judge of his people. When he does this, he cannot but cast himself into the role of one who excommunicates, one who penalizes. This could be based upon the presupposition that he himself is without sin. Yet he may know himself to be a sinner and still have the responsibility of helping to quarantine and localize a person who is more of a threat to the community at that time than he is. Jesus refused the role of a sinless judge on more than one occasion and set himself in opposition to its Pharisaic protagonists. When the rich young ruler called him a *good* teacher, he said: "Why do you call me good? No one is good but God alone" (Mark 10:18). When the die of judgment had been cast and the adulterous woman was to be stoned, Jesus did not raise a question as to the validity of the law, but asked that the one without sin cast the first stone. This passage does not appear in the earliest manuscripts of the Greek. However, its appearance in the later manuscripts may be indicative of efforts on the part of spiritually sensitive Christians of the day of its introduction to reject the penal use of the Bible, because Pharisaism as a social reality had begun to reappear in Christian garb. As Nietzsche says, " The good *must* be Pharisees — they have no choice " (*Thus Spake Zarathustra,* III, lvi, 26).

Yet Jesus, on the other hand, was spiritually secure enough to let most people convict themselves, as he also did the rich young ruler. This was a part of his pastoral care of people. Jesus knew that life itself is the therapist that never asks whether or not a person can bear its treatment. K. E. Kirk, in his evaluation of the relative merits of the penal use of the Bible and the Church as opposed to the pastoral use of them, says:

" It is almost superfluous to ask which of these two methods conforms most closely to the mind of the Good Shepherd. He who broke not the bruised reed, nor quenched the smoking flax, who consorted with publicans and sinners, who bade the apostles to forgive seventy times seven — whosoever came to him, though they fell away and came back again time after time, he would in no wise cast out. How he could do this without lowering his standards, abating his demands, or compromising with evil, is his own peculiar secret. The Church must learn it if and as she can; but her best efforts to put it into effect in the face of the complex demands of the world and the special allurement of the devil have been blind and blundering as compared with his " (*op. cit.,* p. 468).

If a pastor is an authoritarian, penal disciplinarian, however, he has no choice in the kind of relationship he has to many seriously disturbed people. They either never come to him at all or he tends to cut himself off from them when they do. For this reason, the matter of the Biblical knowledge of a minister

and the matter of his approach to interpretation of the Scriptures cannot be separated from his role and function as a pastoral counselor.

Even the more flexible pastor, however, who does seek to
use the Bible pastorally rather than penally, has people come
to him who are sorely troubled by certain recurrent and difficult passages of Scripture. These persons tend to have harsh and
unrelenting judgments upon themselves; their concern for the
meaning of these Scriptures is charged with almost an obsessive kind of anxiety. History and our counseling experience
teach us, in these particular instances, that the penal use of
these Scriptures has failed miserably. As K. E. Kirk says again:

"Penal discipline has always defeated its own ends . . . It has
failed openly . . . That is perhaps the best that can be hoped for;
at least the ground is kept open for the emergence of a pastoral
discipline adequate to cope with the needs of human souls" (*ibid.*).

The pastor's task (with whatever help we can give each other
in the search for the mind of Christ) is to devise for himself a
pastoral discipline in the use of these Scriptures that is "adequate to cope with the needs of human souls." Such a discipline, to be adequate, would involve an adequate interpretation
through a thorough contextual knowledge of the Scripture, and
an adequate technique of pastoral care and personal counseling
through clinical experience with "human souls" who actually
have the problems referred to in the Scripture. The average
minister has been accustomed to interpreting Scripture in the
fashion of the scribes: on the basis of literary evidence and ecclesiastical dogma only. But pastors have only feebly approached
the interpretation of the Scripture by means of clinical histories
and interview records. Their contacts with the needs of the
human beings who present these problems should give some
index to a life-centered interpretation. This was most often the
approach to interpretation that Jesus used, and a pastor does

not get help *directly* from other pastors in his task of devising a pastoral use of the Bible adequate to cope with human needs. He gets this help directly as he relates himself to Jesus of Nazareth and to the troubles of his people as they see them and must bear them. He cannot be bothered too much about what other people think, and what some other scribe such as myself has to say. I can be of only *indirect* help to my reader in his search for the mind of Christ in human suffering.

Nevertheless, I should like to choose five passages of Scripture that pose " legal difficulties " most often to the people who come to me for pastoral counseling. I choose these passages, not because they are the only such passages, but because they appear most often and tend to be the most difficult of the passages that " come up " into the conscious concern of parishioners.

## 1. HOSTILITY

The first passage is found in Matt. 5:21-26:

" ' You have heard that it was said to the men of old, " You shall not kill; and whoever kills shall be liable to judgment." But I say to you that every one who is angry with his brother shall be liable to judgment; whoever insults his brother shall be liable to the council, and whoever says, " You fool! " shall be liable to the hell of fire. So if you are offering your gift at the altar, and there remember that your brother has something against you, leave your gift there before the altar and go; first be reconciled to your brother, and then come and offer your gift. Make friends quickly with your accuser, while you are going with him to court, lest your accuser hand you over to the judge, and the judge to the guard, and you be put in prison; truly, I say to you, you will never get out till you have paid the last penny.' "

These words are quoted to the pastor by a person who is struggling with strong inner motives of hostility which he cannot recognize because of inner blindness, and which he cannot

accept because to do so would mean that he would either have
to express them toward the people whom he resents, reconcile
himself to a peaceful relationship with these persons, or turn
these hostilities back in upon himself in the form of self-
condemnation. The person takes the passage and interprets its
meaning legally. He will say to the pastor, " If you have *any* re-
sentment, you are a murderer." Christ's words are taken literally as if he were enacting that the angry man be tried right
then as a criminal. If this were true, it means that he was in-
troducing a more merciless legalism than that of the Pharisees
whose legalism he was trying to supersede.

Rather, his meaning must be interpreted in the light of the
whole Sermon on the Mount, and more particularly in the light
of the paragraph in which it appears. Such an interpretation
would indicate that (1) Jesus was accepting the fact that people
*do* get angry. (2) Jesus was teaching that anger, and not murder, is the point at which to *begin* the discipline of the heart.
To wait until it has reached the overt act of murder is to give
anger its way until it is too late. Thomas a Kempis, with clear
psychological perception, marks out this interpretation:

" We know not oftentimes what we are able to do, but temptation shows us what we are . . . Wherefore one (Ovid, *Lib.* xiii.
*De Remed. Am.*): 'Withstand the beginnings; the remedy is
applied too late, when the evil has grown strong through long de-
lay.' For first there cometh to the mind a bare thought of evil, then
a strong imagination thereof, afterwards delight, and evil motion,
and then evil consent."

To confuse oneself by saying, however, that anger and murder are the same, apart from the growing process in time toward the full-grownness of sin, is to confuse sin with temptation and to substitute an internal legalism for an external
legalism which is doubly harmful in its effects on human personality. Therefore, such a thing is alien to the mind of Christ,

who gave his life for ours. Sin only when it is full-grown brings
death, in this case. But Jesus is calling attention to the growing
process involved in sin (James 1:15), and the necessity of dealing with hostility at its roots early in its life. Jesus is pointing
to the prevention of crime rather than the punishment of
criminals. (3) Jesus teaches clearly and plainly that anger
should be accepted as anger quickly, and not allowed to fester
into the plots, the plans, the persecutions of a deluded mind.
(4) Jesus teaches that anger is a dangerous emotion, having the
possibilities of destruction in it, not only for oneself, but also
for others. As Alfred Adler says, it is one of the " disjunctive
emotions." For this very reason it must be accepted for what it
is; it must be accepted quickly and dealt with soon through the
process of reconciliation, *before* it becomes something very
much more different and dangerous. And what is that something? It is contempt for the basic personality of the one against
whom one feels hostile. As James says, this contempt becomes
a sort of backbiting venom, and with the tongue we bless God
and we curse men, who " are made in the likeness of God "
(James 3:9).

For these very reasons the persons who come to a pastor with
deep hostile feelings have a *fear* of their own hostile feelings
which is reflected in a contemptuous abhorrence of those whom
they resent. The hallmark of their trouble is that they have held
within themselves, unaccepted, repressed, and unrecognized
feelings which have cankered into systematized persecution
complexes. Jesus is accurately describing the sickening repres-
sion of hostile feelings here.

I quite agree with Frieda Fromm-Reichmann in her penetrat-
ing psychological analysis of her patients and our culture. She
says that we have much more trouble accepting, recognizing,
and learning how to handle our hostile impulses than we do
our sexual impulses. The person with this difficulty comes to

the pastor, and uses the words of Jesus in a *legalistic* way, condemning others in a *hostile* way for their anger toward him. He says that " no Christian would act that way," and that " he does not feel angry toward anyone," because " he just won't let himself think such things." Nevertheless he is consumed in unhappiness, and in bondage to his conflict with the other person.

Or, on the other hand, another type of person with a " saccharine sweetness " and a grandiose feeling of martyrdom will come and say in a rather " otherworldly " sort of way that he or she has nothing but an " absolutely prayerful and perfect love " for another person who has done him a gross injustice. He may even say that he is glad that his soul is free from danger of the judgment because he does not have any hatred. The pastor who has eyes to see and ears to hear will soon sense that such persons are " protesting too much." Fundamentally they are filled with unaccepted and repressed feelings of hostility. The pastor's task is that of bringing them into the awareness, acceptance, and understanding of a conscious sense of personal responsibility. He will find that if he uses a permissive, accepting, and tender listening ministry, a person tends to relax and recognize his real self.

The truth of the whole matter is that a person cannot love his enemy until he has been able to recognize that he *is* his enemy, and *how* and *why* he is his enemy. The only other recourse than this is the repressive legalism of Pharisaism which washes the outside of the cup clean and leaves the inner cup dirty. It resolves itself into basic contempt for personality, and a hellish misery as a result.

## 2. Sexual Desire

Again, let us take the passage found in Matt. 5:27–30:

" 'You have heard that it was said, " You shall not commit adultery." But I say to you that every one who looks at a woman lustfully has already committed adultery with her in his heart. If your right eye causes you to sin, pluck it out and throw it away; it is better that you lose one of your members than that your whole body be thrown into hell. And if your right hand causes you to sin, cut it off and throw it away; it is better that you lose one of your members than that your whole body go into hell.' "

This passage is regularly quoted to the counseling pastor to mean that the very appearance of *any* sexual thought and feeling is the equivalent of adultery. The chaplains of many State hospitals have seen this passage most gruesomely interpreted literally by a patient who actually did " pluck his eye out," because it caused him to see sexual objects. It is difficult for the Biblical legalist to avoid this grotesque caricature of psychological legalism.

The same principles are involved in this passage of Scripture as it appears in the troubled consciousness of counselees that are involved in the passage just preceding it which refers to anger. Quite regularly a pastor of teen-age Christians will have them ask him what this passage means. When he seeks *their* answer which prompted the question, he finds that they feel that for them to have *any* sexual feelings at all is wrong. They interpret the passage legalistically to mean that the very appearance of any sexual thoughts in their conscious minds, particularly dreams and half-waking states, condemns them as " adulterers." I have had young people come to me confessing the act of adultery, and when the true story was out, they had simply called themselves adulterers after having had the first surges of sexual concern awakened within them in the beginning of their mating intentions. No overt behavior was evident.

Following the previously stated pattern of interpretation, we could say that Jesus accepts in the above statement the fact that people do have sexual feelings, that these feelings are the point at which to begin discipline upon the basis of honest recognition and acceptance of one's sexual nature, and not at the act of adultery. To do so is to *prevent* adultery, rather than to *punish* adulterers. He is pastoral in his concern rather than penal. Likewise, also, he teaches that the sexual urge has the capacity of ruling the whole life of the individual, and thus becoming a spiritual tyrant in the life, casting the whole of the life into the fires of passion and destroying it thereby.

The pastoral procedure here is one of radical nature in the counsel of Jesus. He makes the same decision about the sexual passion here that a surgeon makes about a wounded member of the body. If an injured knee threatens the whole life of the individual, the surgeon advises amputation. It is better to lose one member of the body than that the whole life be lost. This is essentially the wisdom of Jesus, therefore, that if the sexual need has become the ruling passion of the whole life, at all times and all places, it would be better not to have it at all. Naturally this is an extreme case, used to demonstrate the ordinary situation. The use of hyperbole as a means of teaching is common in Jesus' words. The choice here is between the lesser of two evils, as in the case of the surgeon, and Jesus is evaluating which would be better.

This interpretation must be placed in the context of the larger teaching of the Sermon on the Mount. Jesus reiterates again and again that the Heavenly Father should be one's God; that one cannot serve God and mammon, otherwise he will be double-minded; and that only the pure in heart can see God. Neither a systematized contempt for one's brother nor a deification of sex can take God's place in one's life without leaving him in danger of total personality disintegration and disorder. A spirit of eagerness toward reconciliation and a subordination of the basic hungers for food and for sex to the sovereign Lordship of Christ are the narrow path between libertinism and mental illness.

How, then, can the pastor implement such a pastoral interpretation of the teachings of Jesus in his counseling ministry
with a person who is struggling with the management of his
sexual strivings?

A class of women in a missionary training school invited a
woman from the local maternity home for unmarried mothers
to speak on the social problem and care of unmarried mothers.
The woman was a major in the Salvation Army. During the
question period, the students asked her: " How should we *start*
to deal with a girl who has become pregnant out of wedlock
who comes to us for help? " She answered, " You should begin
by accepting yourself as a sexual person, coming to understand
your own womanliness, and realizing that the thing that has
happened to this girl might have happened to you! " Georges
Bernanos, in his *Diary of a Country Priest* (p. 155. The Macmillan Company, 1937. Used by permission), epitomizes our
attitudinal orientation:

"I ought never to have received Mlle. Chantal the day before
yesterday. Her first visit to the presbytery was hardly conventional.
And at least I ought to have interrupted her sooner, but as usual
I followed my own impulse. I refused to see anything else but the
girl before me, tottering as though on the brink of a double gulf
of hate and despair. O agonized face! Such a face can never have
lied, such anguish . . . and yet other agonies have not managed to
arouse such pity in me. Why should this pain have such an intoler-
able challenge? My memories of unhappy childhood are still too
vivid, I feel. I, too, experienced once this terrified shrinking from
all the sorrow and shame of life . . . God! such revelations of
impurity would prove the most ordinary tests, if only they did
not show us ourselves. That hideous voice, never yet heard, wakes
in us its long murmuring echo.

"And what then? I ought simply to have acted with all the
more prudence and discretion. Yet instead I hit out right and
left at the risk of wounding . . . while I struck the ravening
beast . . . its defenseless innocent prey. *No priest worthy of the
name sees only the concrete instance.*"

Granted such an understanding of his own personality, the pastor's best approach to the person who presents the teachings in the above-named passage is to hear the person out without rejection or curiosity in his response. The person may use the Scriptures as a means of avoiding the acceptance of the sexual feelings at all. He may use them as a means of justifying his libertinism on the ground that Jesus' teachings are too ideal for him, and that " even preachers don't live up to that ideal." The simplest point of technique is that the pastor shall discover *the particular disturbance in the interpersonal relationships* that caused the person to come to him with the question in the first place. This takes the problem out of the academic sphere and puts it into the sphere of the intimately personal. The pastor discovers this by refusing to interpret the Scripture too quickly until he has some understanding of the context of interpersonal relationships from which the person is speaking. This is a rule of thumb in all questions concerning Biblical interpretation. *Something* caused the person to become concerned about the Scripture. What was it? After a thorough clarification of these factors has been made, the pastor can follow the same procedures of counseling as are suggested in the next chapter on the use of the Bible in interpretation. Suffice it to say that the Scripture should not be used to manipulate the person into a decision that he cannot understand or carry through.

### 3. Divorce

More frequent, however, are the counseling contacts of a pastor with persons involved in a divorce situation. These persons bring the difficult teachings of the Bible on the subject of divorce to their pastor. The variations of teaching in the Bible in Deut. 24:1-4; Mark 10:2-12; Matt. 5:31, 32; Matt. 19:9; and I Cor., ch. 7, are sufficiently wide to need careful exegetic work in order to find clarification. Luther's "plain meaning" of the Scripture does not seem to explain these passages, and the obvious interpretations given by legalists leave the pastor with no recourse in counseling divorced people but almost to excommunicate them from their own personal fellowship as well as from that of the church of which they are members. Excerpts from a letter that I received from a young woman who had been divorced and yet took the claims of the teachings of Jesus seriously state the issues involved in the interpretation of these Scriptures:

"I talked with you last year about having lost my home. . . . I have tried to come to some conclusions and wonder if you will tell me some things now, please.

"It seems to me that all sins except one are forgiven and blotted out and we are given another chance. Is this for me now, too? And if so, then what do the verses about marriage and divorce that bother me so mean?

"Now if nothing happens, I plan to marry next spring. . . . This is ideal, but many ideals which are or must be wrong still bother me.

"I realize my teaching to prepare me for dates at sixteen was not graduated to prepare me for the beauty and sacredness of marriage later. This bothered us when I was married and he said he wondered if it was right. Now, being divorced, I do wonder, too.

"Ever since I can remember, I have heard of girls who were ruined for life. I never thought what they did after this. To me this makes life a burden. Yet, if I could discard this idea, I can forget what has happened.

"Please excuse this. I know that this should have been learned years ago and people's wrong ideas sound stupid. But these have worried me for years, and I suppose they will until I can replace them with the right thoughts.

"Respectfully yours."

The point of contention concerning the teachings of Jesus is not about divorce itself in our present situation, but primarily about the problem of remarriage after the divorce has been granted. This is precisely the point at which the young woman who wrote me the above letter was concerned. It is fitting that we work on the problem of Scriptural interpretation, and then give the letter which I wrote in response to the letter from which I have quoted.

The passages that are taken from the teachings of Jesus give the interpreter most of the counseling situations. The Deuteronomy reference is from the Jewish law, but the teachings of Jesus are the single example of an outright, specific prohibition concerning a definite social act to be found in his teaching. Research in the writings of ethical teachers of contemporary Christendom, particularly Protestantism, reveals that they tend to agree at two or three points in the interpretation of Jesus' teachings concerning divorce and remarriage. (1) They agree that Jesus was aiming his teaching primarily at the improvement of the treatment of women in his day, when women had no legal rights at all and were considered as the chattels of the men to whom they were bound by marriage. This is a totally different social situation from that of contemporary American life, in which the woman actually has a greater legal advantage in our courts of divorce. In his day adultery was a crime committed *by a woman,* not ordinarily by a man. Hence, only a man could initiate divorce procedures. It is interesting, therefore, that Jesus says, " Everyone that looks upon a *woman* ... . to lust after her, has committed adultery with her in *his* heart " (Paul Ramsey, *Basic Christian Ethics.* Charles Scribner's Sons, 1950). (2) They tend to agree that, as Emil Brunner says, " the moral presuppositions of divorce, in contradistinction to the legal presuppositions, can be codified in no law " (*The Divine Imperative,* p. 362. The Westminster Press, 1947). And, as F. R. Barry says, " the legal tie [of marriage] corresponds no longer to any moral or spiritual realities " (F. R.

Barry, *Christianity and the New World,* p. 235. Harper & Brothers, 1932).

The pastor can no more successfully reduce to law Jesus' teaching, " You, therefore, must be perfect, as your heavenly Father is perfect." Nevertheless, that inability does not invalidate, but intensifies the validity of the teaching as being eternal and unchangeable, even though time and circumstance always make our pastoral application of the ideal imperfect. K. E. Kirk again helps us in our dilemma by saying:

" The Church must always and everywhere set before men the highest standards she knows in conduct . . . but she must be slow to enforce them by confining her membership to those who acquiesce. The shepherd's staff and not the tyrant's sword must be her true weapon. The whole flock is to be led into the fold, not the few harried into it whilst the many are left to their fate " (*op. cit.,* p. 469).

As Brunner helpfully suggests, the pastor here " must recognize how human sinfulness and weakness make the order relative. For in spite of our fundamental scruples, actually in most cases remarriage is . . . the one which corresponds more closely to the ideal, than to remain unmarried, not merely for the widowed, but also for the divorced " (*op. cit.,* p. 363).

Here again I am fully aware that concurrence in the opinions of these writers implies that we are dealing with the whole problem of the purpose of the Church in the world. We are faced with the alternative of defining our task as pastors and leading our churches to accept a more creative and less defensive approach to their task. We have two alternatives: We can define our task as that of aiding weak and sinful people to be pure in heart so that they may see God. Or, we can define our task as that of drawing up a moral code, legally stated with exactness, by means of which we may *exclude* the weak and sinful and *include* the strong and righteous. The Spirit of Christ gives life, illuminates history, and makes the letter redemptive, but the letter of the law, left unaided, kills.

Such a conclusion pushes us to a more creative solution of the problem that the divorcee who is concerned deeply about the mind of Christ presents. The minister begins to look for the causes of the divorce rather than the symptoms. In doing this, he does not seek to determine the " innocent party," but leaves that for the divorce court lawyers to determine. Rather, he seeks to understand the whole pattern of interrelationships that conspire together to shake the intentions of a married couple away from permanent union in happiness. He asks such questions of a couple as: " How is it that you came to know each other? " " Did you have any premarital instruction concerning the character and purpose of a Christian marriage? " " How long did you know each other before your marriage? " " How did your parents feel about your getting married the first time? " " What sort of guidance did your pastor give you before you were married? " Then he finds out that everyone has sinned in the conspiracy of blind impulse and base ignorance of a whole community, and that not even the church can throw the first stone in the judgment of adultery or any other sin. All of this is particularly true if the church defines its task and that of its minister as that of throwing stones.

With these considerations in mind, let me say that in counseling divorcees who are contemplating remarriage, I am primarily concerned with three issues: First, I am concerned with their basic attitudes toward the Christian way of life itself. I pay attention to the way in which they have been able to profit from their past mistakes, to accept personal responsibility for their own part of the marital failure, and express this in terms of Christian repentance and rededication. Many of these persons have no connection at all with the Church, and most of them have only a nominal connection. A few of them, tragically enough, have been faithfully religious. Whatever they consider themselves to be religiously, however, I consider to be primary in terms of prognosis of their proposed remarriage. Secondly, I consider their willingness to participate in a definite program of instruction in marriage and family living given under my own personal guidance and extending over a period of several weeks. This program includes personal counseling, Biblical interpretation, reading assignment and discussion, and medical referral. Thirdly, I consider the possibilities of the couple's becoming a part of a helpful fellowship of other Christians who will sustain and support them in securing the foundations of the marriage.

In brief, I consider the couple who have one or both contracting parties remarrying after divorce in the same way I would consider any other couple who seek to marry: in terms of their basic Christian commitment, their degree of preparation for marriage, and their partaking of the fellowship of Christians. Such an approach is on the basis of the future and not the past, their resources and not their liabilities, and their hopes and not their fears.

The whole approach of a pastor to the divorcee who plans to remarry should be the alignment of his counsel in the direction of the creative possibilities that the person has for future realization of abundant living. The pastor here becomes a shepherd whose mission is that of counseling with the wounded ones in order " that they may have life, and have it abundantly " (John 10:10). " God . . . has qualified us to be ministers of a new covenant, not in a written code but in the Spirit; for the written code kills, but the Spirit gives life " (II Cor. 3:5, 6).

It was with something of this background that I answered the letter quoted earlier in this discussion in the following way:

" Dear Miss —————:

" I received your kind letter several days ago. I wish that I could talk to you personally about the extremely difficult problem which you presented. The letter which I am writing is a very inadequate way of dealing with the problem but I shall do the best I can.

" I believe that whether you are married again or whether you stay single, you will always have to carry a sense of failure with reference to your former marriage. In this sense you will not have the degree of happiness or fulfillment in life that you would have had if you and your husband had not made a failure of your first marriage. I think that there is a great deal of happiness in the world for you if you are willing to accept the fact that you have made mistakes in the past and that things never will be quite the same because of that.

" In your feeling toward God you seem to feel that having been divorced is an unpardonable thing. I grant you that the direct message of Jesus' teaching on this subject, *if read literally and apart from the Spirit of Christ might give you half a reason for believing this.* All that I can do to reassure you is to say that I do not believe that Jesus meant for you to get the impression that you have, any more than he would want you to blame your failures on anybody else.

" I cannot tell you what to do in this lonely valley of decision through which you are walking, but I can remind you of the assurance of my own friendship and understanding, and of the providential love and care of our Christlike God. We know in part and we prophesy in part. You are looking through a glass darkly, but if you are faithful to the belief in the all-inclusive love of Christ, you shall sooner or later know even as you are known by him. In these decisions we know not how to pray as we ought to pray, but my prayer is that the Spirit who searches your heart will cause you to know for yourself what is right and give you security in your own decisions. Whatever decision you make, I want to remind you, will not affect the understanding sincerity with which I have expressed my friendship to you. You will most certainly have my sensitive appreciation. This is the only way that I have of showing you how I think God feels about you.

" Let me hear from you as to what you do and keep in mind not only the words of Jesus but the Spirit of Jesus. I am keenly interested to know about the person whom you plan to marry. I hope that he is just the kind of person who is capable of helping you to manage your feelings and to encourage you in the ways that only a husband can encourage a woman. By all means, I hope that he is a Christian with a deep personal experience of God's grace.

" With kindest personal regards, I am,

" Sincerely yours."

## 4. HOMOSEXUALITY

Another series of Scripture passages that pose thorny problems to the minister as he counsels disturbed persons is that series concerning homosexuality. The passage in Gen., ch. 13 concerning Sodom and Gomorrah and the passages of Paul in Rom. 1:26–32 and I Cor. 6:9 are occasionally presented to the pastor by persons whose homosexual needs have become a serious threat to their total way of life.

" For this reason God gave them up to dishonorable passions. Their women exchanged natural relations for unnatural, and the men likewise gave up natural relations with women and were consumed with passion for one another, men committing shameless acts with men and receiving in their own persons the due penalty for their error.

" And since they did not see fit to acknowledge God, God gave them up to a base mind and to improper conduct. They were filled with all manner of wickedness, evil, covetousness, malice. Full of envy, murder, strife, deceit, malignity, they are gossips, slanderers, haters of God, insolent, haughty, boastful, inventors of evil, disobedient to parents, foolish, faithless, heartless, ruthless. Though they know God's decree that those who do such things deserve to die, they not only do them but approve those who practice them " (Rom. 1:26–32).

" Do you not know that the unrighteous will not inherit the kingdom of God? Do not be deceived; neither the immoral, nor idolaters, nor adulterers, nor homosexuals, . . . will inherit the kingdom of God " (I Cor. 6:9, 10).

The pastor again is pushed into a judicial corner by the literalistic interpretation of the passage in which these persons are described as individuals whom even God himself has " given up," and who, therefore, are lost and without hope in the world, incapable of entering the Kingdom of God. The patient described in Chapter I who came to the State hospital feeling that God had given him up to a reprobate mind was concerned at this point because he perceived himself as being a " homosexual."

From the point of view of the Hebrew mind, any type of sexual behavior that threatened the perpetuity of the race and did not issue, therefore, in the birth of children was an abomination before God. They took seriously the command to be fruitful and multiply. This feeling is rooted deep in the primitive unconscious, according to my own way of interpretation, of modern society. It is so powerful that a severe taboo is laid somewhat blindly and unreasoningly upon homosexuality. The student of primitive religions alone can enter into the real strength of the meaning of taboo to a clan of people.

Furthermore, overt homosexuality, in the time of the Roman Empire, was a symbol of the Greek way of life, in which it was socially acceptable. The open hostility of the Hebrew mind to all Hellenism gravitates to this taboo also, and adds to the strength of the Pauline condemnation of homosexuality.

But, more specifically, the record says that the homosexuals not only practice this behavior themselves but pervert the youth of their community by teaching others to do so also. This made the threat to the safety of the children of responsible parents more acute. They did not want their children perverted to this practice and were willing to take drastic steps to prevent it, with only secondary regard for the personality of the person who did it.

These same forces, in a different context, are at work in the modern condemnation of this particular type of sexuality. The strong taboo against the " unnaturalness " of it roots deeply in the continuing need of the race to be perpetuated in children. Homosexuality is a parentally irresponsible way of being sexual. Then, too, homosexuality, as has been revealed by the Kinsey studies, is a type of sexuality that tends to be characteristic of upper social level groups and abhorrent to lower social level groups, although no easy generalization can be made here. A part of the lashing condemnation that strikes out at the person who is homosexually active is motivated by this cultural clash of deeper feelings.

But more particularly the pastor, who is the minister of reconciliation between community interests for the protection of the younger people in the community, on the one hand, and the excruciating agony of a homosexual person who cannot seem to make his or her sexual behavior conform to community standards, is faced by the grim social reality that the ninety-nine in this case must be protected from the one. Yet he must, according to his role as a good shepherd, minister also to the one in a redemptive manner. This is the pastor's dilemma.

Of course, the pastor needs to bear in mind that many of the people who come to him concerned about homosexual feelings, applying the condemnation of the above-quoted Scriptures to themselves, are not criminals confirmed in so-called perverted habits. They are persons who are sincerely concerned about their latent tendencies in these directions. Here the pastor can serve a vital ministry of prevention if he has taken the trouble to train himself in the principles and practice of formal counseling. If he has not disciplined himself in this way, he needs to seek some pastor who has had that type of training and to enlist his aid in the pastoral care of the person with the problem. This is not a type of difficulty to be handled superficially or by " rule of thumb " common-sense advice. A certain amount of psychiatric information is necessary. The person may even need the help of a psychiatrist, as most certainly was true of the person referred to in Chapter I.

It is my guidance to the person concerned, however, about the meaning of the particular passages of Scripture quoted here that the Scripture is not referring to the person who is genuinely disturbed and unhappy over his condition. The Scripture is referring to persons who *prefer* their way of life to any other, who delight in being just as they are, and who actually seek to teach their way of life to others as being the ideal. This is clearly evident in the first chapter of Romans. Ordinarily this type of person does not seek counsel from a pastor or anyone else, except in those cases in which he is using the counseling interview as a means of getting sexual stimulation from talking with a person of the same sex, or in those cases in which he has been " jilted " by one of his homosexual partners, or in those cases in which he is about to be caught or has been caught by the community authorities on charges of which he is actually guilty. Such an interpretation as this only alleviates but does not solve the problem the person has. However, it may help the person to disentangle his feeling toward himself from that which God really feels toward him. As A. A. Gross has said, " it is clearly the duty of the clergyman to make the homosexual see that there are no untouchables in the Kingdom of God." He can partially do this by clearing up questions as to the Biblical teachings in the way that I have suggested here, and by pointing to the more hopeful aspects of the Biblical teachings. Our main objective here is to clear up the confused attitudes concerning the Bible and its message, because such attitudes may easily block out any other help the pastor seeks to render.

For more specific guidance on this problem, the pastor may consult the following literature:

A. A. Gross, " The Homosexual in Society," in *Pastoral Psychology,*
  April, 1950.
Russell L. Dicks, " The Problem of a Homosexual Theology Stu-
  dent," in *Pastoral Psychology,* May, 1950.
Alfred C. Kinsey, *et al., Sexual Behavior in the Human Male.*
  W. B. Saunders, 1948.

## 5. The Unpardonable Sin

Finally, another illustration of the ethical dilemma into
which a pastor is thrown by his role as an interpreter of certain
legally stated passages of the Bible is that of the sayings concerning " the unpardonable sin." These are as follows:

" ' But whoever blasphemes against the Holy Spirit never has
forgiveness, but is guilty of an eternal sin ' — for they had said,
' He has an unclean spirit ' " (Mark 3:29, 30).

" ' Therefore I tell you, every sin and blasphemy will be forgiven men, but the blasphemy against the Spirit will not be forgiven. And whoever says a word against the Son of man will be
forgiven; but whoever speaks against the Holy Spirit will not be
forgiven, either in this age or in the age to come ' " (Matt. 12:31,
32).

" ' And every one who speaks a word against the Son of man
will be forgiven; but he who blasphemes against the Holy Spirit
will not be forgiven ' " (Luke 12:10).

" For it is impossible to restore again to repentance those who
have once been enlightened, who have tasted the heavenly gift, and
have become partakers of the Holy Spirit, and have tasted the goodness of the word of God and the powers of the age to come, if
they then commit apostasy, since they crucify the Son of God on
their own account and hold him up to contempt. For land which
has drunk the rain that often falls upon it, and brings forth vegeta-
tion useful to those for whose sake it is cultivated, receives a blessing from God. But if it bears thorns and thistles, it is worthless and
near to being cursed; its end is to be burned " (Heb. 6:4–8).

" For if we sin deliberately after receiving the knowledge of the
truth, there no longer remains a sacrifice for sins, but a fearful
prospect of judgment, and a fury of fire which will consume the

adversaries. A man who has violated the law of Moses dies without mercy at the testimony of two or three witnesses. How much worse punishment do you think will be deserved by the man who has spurned the Son of God, and profaned the blood of the covenant by which he was consecrated, and outraged the Spirit of grace? For we know him who said, 'Vengeance is mine, I will repay.' And again, 'The Lord will judge his people'" (Heb. 10:26-30).

A forty-eight-year-old man came to his pastor saying that he felt that he had committed the unpardonable sin, and that he could never be saved. He refused to talk about anything but this idea and seemed to be so obsessed by it that no amount of religious reassurance or ethical instruction comforted his heart or guided him through his confused perspective of life. This is particularly strange in that he had hitherto lived an exemplary life as a public-school teacher, as a regular attendant at church, as a Bible teacher in a men's Bible class, and as a deacon in his church. The pastor's reassurance of the man was to no avail, but the verses quoted above were repeatedly quoted by the man. The explanations of the pastor seemed only to confuse him further. He became so upset that he could not work, but stayed at home pacing the floor and becoming more and more tense, sleepless, and refusing to eat. The pastor was baffled as to how to deal with the problem, and none of the man's many religious counselors was able to meet his needs.

The passages listed above are most often quoted by persons who are compulsively obsessed with the idea of being irretrievably "lost." They are characteristic of what Bergston calls "symptomatic religiosity." No amount of reassurance suffices to relieve their complaint, and no amount of interpretation clarifies their mind. The end result of a legalistic approach to the use of the Bible is put into bold caricature in such persons. Their situation represents the compulsive disintegration of super-legalism. The power of the compulsive works through the legalistic use of these passages and makes the compulsive obsession all the more powerful.

Historical perspective and information offer the most understandable explanation of these procedures. The experience of the Early Church can also be compared to that of contemporary sects of perfectionism. Members of the community from which the New Testament was born were so firmly convinced of the completely radical change effected by a profession of faith in Christ and the utter pointlessness of *any* deviation from the ethics of the Church (particularly in the prospect of an immediate return of the Lord) that they saw no possibility of any kind of repentance after baptism. John T. McNeill gives further guidance at this point:

"In documents of the second and third centuries we see evidence of divergence of opinion with respect to the discipline of offenders. The temper of the Church, confronted by the moral laxity of the contemporary pagan society, was stern toward those who violated Christian standards of behavior. There was much hesitation even about admitting to repentance and reconciliation those who had committed the grave sins of idolatry, unchastity, and the shedding of blood. Some writers — remembering the language in Matt. (ch. 12:31, 32), and Mark (ch. 3:28–30) about the sin for which there is no forgiveness, or the stern warning in Heb. (ch. 12:15–17) concerning Esau who having sold his birthright 'found no chance to repent, though he sought it with tears,' or the reference in I John 5:16 to a sin unto death for which prayer is not recommended — held that these were unpardonable, or 'irremissible,' sins, for which the Church had no warrant to take any action leading to the sinner's restoration. But opinion varied. Tertullian, writing shortly before 200, and Origen (d. 253) are numbered among the rigorous disciplinarians, while Hermas (ca. 125) permits the restoration of an apostate and of an adulteress, and Clement of Alexandria (ca. 200) represents the apostle John as pardoning a repentant bandit. The difference here is part of the whole problem of qualifications for church fellowship, aspects of which later gave rise to the Novatianist and the Donatist schisms. The motive of protecting the fellowship from pollution was in tension with the motive of restoring the sinful brother. Gradually the more liberal interpretation prevailed, and as the penitential discipline was systematized it ultimately made provision for the reception of those guilty of the gravest offenses " (*The History of the Cure of Souls,* p. 89. Harper & Brothers, 1951).

Out of these stringent difficulties in interpretation grew the ancient practice of " clinical baptism," by which a person did not become a " professing " Christian until shortly before his death, lest he be forever excommunicated if by chance or intention he should " slip " once. The contemporary multiplication of " Holy Roller " sects among the extremely underprivileged and the cults among the privileged, the development of humanistic religions such as psychoanalysis, and the growth of communities of misery of " fellowships of the nameless damned " among alcoholics, divorcees, and homosexuals, are social phenomena that can partially be explained by the way in which the " out-groups," excluded by the church, tend to develop healing communities of their own.

The unpardonable sin idea usually reflects the gnawing depths of the person's feeling of chasm between himself and the particular community of faith in which he has had confidence and upon whose approval he is dependent. It may or may not reflect a particular act or series of acts that he has committed. More often it represents an inner sense of estrangement arising out of deep and long-term emotional deprivation of his need for affection and security. It may be a symptom of his refusal to accept his finite limitations as a human being, and his low frustration tolerance in accepting the limitations that all people have to bear.

Of course, the interpretation of the real meaning which Jesus had in mind is made clear by Major, Manson, and Wright when they say that these words have needlessly troubled " many sensitive consciences." " These words are not directed against sins of unbelief or sins of sensuality but against the malignant moral blindness which deliberately affirms that that which is good is evil " (*The Mission and Message of Jesus,* p. 65. E. P. Dutton & Co., Inc., 1938). Clinical experience reveals that *these* people do not come to counselors, pastors, and other professional persons with problems of guilt. The deadliness of their sin is that they are not aware of it.

These imposing ethical dilemmas of the ways in which the Bible appears clinically in the stream of consciousness of the pastor's counselees are enough to discourage him profoundly. When the pastor as a teacher sows legalism to the wind, he and his successors need expect nothing but a whirlwind of ethical confusion in their counseling ministries. In order to perform the paradoxical function, the pastor, at the risk of being misunderstood by the more legalistic members of his flock, must forego the self-preservative comforts afforded the legalist. He must accept the social responsibilities that come with the kind of Biblical interpretation that seeks the spirit rather than the letter of the Scripture, its meaning and purpose rather than merely its language and symbols, because the one gives life and the other kills and destroys. Sin takes advantage of the situation of the legalist and beguiles the mind and makes sin all the more sinful, and when it is full-grown brings death.

CHAPTER III

## THE BIBLE IN THE PASTORAL
## CARE OF CHILDREN

PASTORS are called as healers and comforters of adults
whose spirits have been stunted, twisted, and maimed by
inept and ill-intentioned persons who have sought to teach
them the Bible. The more deeply the pastor feels this sense of
mission and the more often he is pressed into the task of caring
for these confused people, the more concerned he becomes
about trying to prevent this from happening in the lives of
those growing children of his flock who are still in the forma-
tive years of their lives.

In many instances, the adult counselees of a pastor have been
alienated from the sources of religious experience by parents
who used religion as a means of forcing conformity to their
own wishes, however just or unjust those wishes may have
been. In this way, religion was rejected by the child in order to
maintain his own personal integrity. Now in adulthood, he
tends to use his parents' mishandling of religion as an excuse
for avoiding the discipline of a more positive search for faith.
Nevertheless, such adults are filled with moral wistfulness.
They yearn for some new and meaningful experience *of their
own*. They crave internal assurance, inner fullness, and spiritual
meaning. They are lonely for a community of comrades who
share meaningfully in a fellowship of belief. In a vital way they
are " religious orphans," who, having been driven out from

their spiritual heritage, "can't go home again" but wander spiritually as fugitives and vagabonds upon the earth.

In other instances these adults find themselves laden with the forms of their family religion, but denied the power of it. They slavishly seek to conform to the teachings of parents and Church (with devious motives for doing so), but develop a secret life of symptoms that they cannot understand or accept. They have been bound with "heavy burdens, hard to bear," which were laid upon their shoulders when they themselves were too young to support themselves economically or to express their emotions verbally. They have been saddled with laws for living without having been afforded the light that comes from patient explanation and tender care of inquiring minds. More than that, they have been deprived of the inspiration that came from unlimited quantities of understanding and affection. Careful study of their personal histories does not reveal either parents or pastors who have moved so much as a finger to help them to carry their load.

As long as a pastor stays safely within the inner circle of the "pillars" of his church, he does not confront such adults too often. But when he gets on the outer fringe of his membership, or when he takes a post as a counselor of college students, as a chaplain in a hospital, or as a military chaplain, he begins to meet them on every hand. The misery that he confronts there causes him to inquire into the kind of use that he, his church school teachers, and especially the parents of growing children are making of the Bible in the development of healthy personalities. He concerns himself with the reasons why the Bible is a "closed book" to so many adults. He works diligently to devise ways and means of keeping its fountains open, whereby God refreshes his children on their pilgrim ways.

## The Bible at the Crossroads of the Spiritual Pilgrimage

In order to discover the reasons why the Bible becomes an offense to many, the pastor needs to look into the personal spiritual pilgrimages of persons who have lost their way. He needs to go back to the crossroads where the individual was misled.

A group of graduate students and I did just this in a program of clinical pastoral training at the Kentucky State Hospital in 1947. We studied the religious histories of 69 acutely mentally ill patients. We discovered that 17.2 per cent of these persons were suffering from long-term moral and religious conflicts (Wayne E. Oates, " The Role of Religion in the Psychoses," *Pastoral Psychology,* May, 1950). Biblical material stood prominently in the delusional pattern of these patients, and a good deal of our time was spent in a program of religious *re*-education with the objective of maturing their religious outlook and encouraging them to disentangle their relationship to God from their morbid relationships to their parents. In about half of the cases we had a modicum of success.

Several great problems arise in the formation of a child's Biblical understanding as this understanding affects his emotional growth. These problems lay the ground for later religious confusion which may necessitate pastoral counseling with the unhappy adult. Careful attention to these possibilities for trouble in the character education stages of a child's development would effectively prevent later religious disturbances and eliminate the necessity of pastoral counseling for many people who grow up under the close supervision of the church.

First, the Bible is used too often by parents and teachers as a means of threatening and punishing a child. As a result the child develops a fear reaction toward the Bible. Instead of literally taking a whip and administering corporal punishment to the child, parents, and even ministers, often take a Bible verse and "threaten and whip" with it. Both methods reveal a spiritually threadbare parent-child relationship. A child who uses bad language is told that the Bible says he is in danger of hell-fire. A child who has done something wrong is called in and told to sit and listen as his parent reads the Bible to him about his wrongdoing. The Bible should *never* be used as a fear-producing instrument for punishing little children.

Secondly, children are often taught goals by parents, teachers, and pastors that are mutually contradictory. Two ideals are taught and given the sanction of infallibility " because they are in the Bible." For instance, they are taught to honor their father and mother, and, from the same Bible, to hate their father and mother for the gospel's sake. Likewise, they are taught the hero-success stories of the Bible alongside the virtues of humility and noncompetitiveness. At different times, ordinarily, they get different impressions. As Gardner Murphy says, " Western culture is shot through and through with the ambivalence that puts its mark on every growing person: Get ahead; don't be forward. Climb to the top; don't climb over others. Heaven helps them that helps themselves; he that saveth his life shall lose it " (*Personality: A Biosocial Approach to Origins and Structure,* p. 579. Harper & Brothers, 1947). During childhood, these paradoxes go unnoticed. But in the normal conflicts of adolescence they become pronounced and acute contradictions. Only the maturity that experience and careful counseling give resolves the tensions in a higher synthesis of understanding. These acute contradictions are regularly presented to counseling pastors by adolescence.

Thirdly, the Bible is often taught to the child by sincere but misinformed church school teachers in such a way as to give him an actually wrong attitude toward the Bible. When, on the basis of wrong information, the child enters a class under a trained teacher, he has to unlearn the misinformation. Devout college professors who teach the Bible to freshmen who have come to their classes from the church schools of their local home churches are concerned about three problems that the students present: First, the student has a bare minimum of factual information about the Bible, even though the content method of teaching has been used since before the child started to public school. College freshmen often are unable simply to locate the accounts of Creation, the Lord's Prayer, and the Twenty-third Psalm. Secondly, the student has no idea of historical perspective in his grasp of the Biblical story. Moses, for example, may be thought of as a contemporary of Jesus, and Isaiah as a close personal friend of the apostle Paul! Thirdly, students have derived pitifully childlike misunderstandings of God from the way in which the Bible has been taught them. For example, all Scriptural passages are ascribed equal validity for moral and religious living. The exhortations about remaining single, for instance, in the teachings of Paul (I Cor. 7:25 ff.) or the teachings of Jesus as to the time of his return (Matt. 24:36) are often placed on a par with their respective teachings about Christian love and the cross. Examples from the life of David are given equal sanction with those from the life of Jesus. When everything becomes of equal importance, the sense of discriminate judgment is lost and nothing tends to matter.

This indicates that the factor which Lewis J. Sherrill calls " stress and neglect " in the use of the Bible " may seriously distort the Bible in the hands of any individual or group." Ralph D. Heim, in an exhaustive study of 50,000 pieces of church school literature from a wide selection of different religious groups, further illustrates the conclusions drawn in the preceding chapter on the legalistic use of the Bible. He discovered that in Christian Church literature, the ten most frequently used New Testament verses taken together are used considerably less than the Ten Commandments; also, he discovered that the Commandments as a group are used with a total frequency considerably above the Beatitudes. "Perhaps there is some reason for some to say that ours is a Ten Commandments Christianity."

The over-all impression that one gets from a study such as that by Professor Heim is that the prophetic genius of both the Old Testament and the New Testament is considerably less in use than are the legalistic formulations of both Testaments ("The Bible in the Literature of Christian Education." Unpublished research).

One of the dangers pastors want to avoid is that of using the Bible as a means of enforcing or "retreading" their own moral convictions, which may not have Biblical foundation but simply reflect community mores. An example of this is a teaching that was given to me as a child in a Sunday school to the effect that Negroes were ordained of God to be a race of servants because of the sin of Ham, the son of Noah! The pastor and lay teachers who are concerned with developing healthy personalities must of necessity pay more attention to the way in which the growing self is conditioned from within and less to the ways in which it is coerced from without. Unconscious forces are at work in the parent-child, teacher-child, pastor-child, and community-child relationship, teaching far more than the verbal exchange of words and ideas can. Children particularly are at work interpreting for themselves, and it is a fact that what they are saying to themselves is far more important than what is being said to them.

This points to a final hazard in the pastoral use of the Bible with growing children and youth in their spiritual pilgrimages. Parents and pastors tend to use the Bible as a means of producing obedience and conformity rather than as a means of "opening up " significant questions and concerns within the spiritual life of the individual that will cause him to confront God *on his own*. Biblical instruction of today grew to its present state of crystallization under the shadow of a mechanistic and behavioristic psychology which is the foundation of secular education in America. The presuppositions of such a pragmatic psychology are that the teacher or the parent *always* knows or *should always* know best for the growing student; the learning process is conceived of as being a " one-way street," so to speak, and the possibility of revelation coming to the teacher from the student is not too often considered. The objective of teaching the Bible, from this point of view, then, is that of producing obedience and conformity to that which the teacher or parent considers best.

In a real sense, the teaching of the Bible, couched in the framework of the earlier and more ancient behaviorism of the Pharisees, has fallen prey to this modern kind of mechanistic attitude. In church and home, the Bible tends to become a tool of such a consciously chosen and applied psychology. Growing persons are *manipulated* by means of the Bible instead of being introduced to it as a book that has authenticity by reason of the reality of the experience of the persons whom it describes and that, therefore, the Bible is capable of speaking for itself through the Holy Spirit in such a way that each person tends to hear it " in his own language."

However, this is not to consign to disuse the experience of personal testimony on the part of parent and pastor. Some parents and pastors, in reaction against the damage done by indoctrination, overlook growing children's needs to know what their parents' and pastors' spiritual pilgrimages have meant to them. A parent or pastor can share those experiences in such a way that the child can know them intimately, without at the same time causing the child to feel that he has to conform to the experience of his parent or pastor in every detail. A conformity-demanding psychology has proved most efficient at producing two types of persons: in the public school it has produced efficient robot personalities, who function without protest in a technological society without feeling and with objectivity as their reward; in the church school, it has produced efficient Pharisees, who function within an ecclesiastical tradition without rebellion and with " respectability " as their reward.

In both the scientific tradition and the ecclesiastical tradition, the psychiatrist and psychoanalyst on the one hand and the counseling pastor on the other serve as a sort of cleanup crew to care for the casualties. These casualties are those who refused or were unable to conform, and were cast out for not doing so, and those who have conformed but have, nevertheless, found their lives drab, empty, meaningless, and driven by unrequited and nameless hungers for something that eludes them constantly. In the meanwhile, they wander to and fro, not knowing who they are or where they are going, with " that one talent which is death to hide " hidden within them. The Kingdom of God is denied its creative birth in the community of mankind.

### The Pastor as a Biblical Teacher Among Growing Students

Practically every pastor who cares for his flock in their times of quiet inner desperation with such problems as have been described here is aware of the issues that I have named. However, it is a point of quiet inner desperation for us ourselves to know what to do about them. Let me venture to suggest a few points at which to begin.

It is obvious that one point at which to begin is in our preaching. Are we as pastors using the Bible as a means of coercing and cajoling, manipulating and using people from the pulpit to " get them to do what we want them to do," to " get them behind us in our plans," to " sell them this or that thing "? Preaching, like counseling, has, or should have, a strong element of sound teaching in it. By sound teaching I do not mean merely the exactness of *what* we teach, but the kind of emotional frame of reference by means of which we communicate in the interpersonal relationship between us and the persons listening.

It is important, therefore, for us as pastors to begin with the psychological frame of reference from which we are operating as preachers of the Bible. The Bible itself has much to offer at this point. At least two distinct psychological approaches to personality are evident in the New Testament. One is that of the legalists, to which reference has been made repeatedly. The Pharisees were the most obvious examples of this type of psychology. They sought to control every act of every hour and at every place in the individual's life. Minute rules were set up intending to canalize human behavior completely. In Christianity another set of rules sprang up, great and small, and became what Tertullian later called " molds " for behavior. The person is overlooked as a participating perceiver in the process of discovering what is good. He may grow up to be an *obedient* person, but one untrained in discovering ethical insights for himself.

The second type of psychology of personality found within the Bible is one of the inner consciousness of selfhood in relation to a feeling of having been sent into the world for a purpose which is ever concealing and revealing itself to us. Moses, when confronted with the meaningful purpose of God, asked, " Who am I, that I should go unto Pharaoh . . . ?" The psalmist, filled with a sense of guilt (for which a purely legalistic psychology has only punishment for a solution), asked that he be made to know " truth in the inward parts; and in the hidden part . . . to know wisdom." Jesus often asked himself who he was, defined again and again his purpose in the world, asked demoniacs who they were, and asked his disciples who it was that men supposed him to be.

Robert Frost states the poignant need for the personal confrontation of these questions on the part of children and adults today in his poem " The Cabin in the Clearing ":

MIST:     I don't believe the sleepers in this house
              Know where they are.
SMOKE: They've been here long enough
              To push the woods back from around the house
              And part them in the middle with a path.
MIST:     And still I doubt if they know where they are.
              And I begin to fear they never will.
              All they maintain the path for is the comfort
              Of visiting with the equally bewildered.
              Nearer in plight their neighbors are than distance.
SMOKE: I am the guardian wraith of starlit smoke
              That leans out this and that way from their chimney.
              I will not have their happiness despaired of.
MIST:     No one — not I — would give them up for lost
              Simply because they don't know where they are.
              I am the damper counterpart of smoke
              That gives off from a garden ground at night
              But lifts no higher than a garden grows.
              I cotton to their landscape. That's who I am.
              I am no further from their fate than they are.
SMOKE: They must by now have learned the native tongue.
              Why don't they ask the Red Man where they are?
MIST:     They often do, and none the wiser for it.
              So do they also ask philosophers
              Who came to look in on them from the pulpit.
              They will ask anyone there is to ask —
              In the fond faith accumulated fact

           Will of itself take fire and light the world up.
           Learning has been a part of their religion.
SMOKE:  If the day ever comes when they know who
           They are, they may know better where they are.
           But who they are is too much to believe —
           Either for them or the onlooking world.
           They are too sudden to be credible.
MIST:    Listen, they murmur talking in the dark
           On what should be their daylong theme continued.
           Putting the lamp out has not put their thought out.
           Let us pretend the dew drops from the eaves
           Are you and I eavesdropping on their unrest —
           A mist and smoke eavesdroping on a haze —
           And see if we can tell the bass from the soprano.
           Than smoke and mist who better could appraise
           The kindred spirit of an inner haze.
(Printed in *The New York Times Book Review*, February 3, 1952.)

Let me recommend the psychological context for preaching, pastoral care, and religious education set forth in the book, by Lewis J. Sherrill, *The Struggle of the Soul*. It offers a ground of meaning in which even the youngest child and oldest adult can participate. He emphasizes the need for a fresh examination of " the career of the human self . . . as it passes through certain major stages, or types of experience, during the journey from the beginning to the end of life " (*op. cit.,* p. 3. The Macmillan Company, 1951). Then he sets himself to the task of describing a Biblical view of the nature of personality as being at its core the emergence of a dynamic self in the unfolding pilgrimage of a meaningful existence in relation to the purpose of God for the individual in the universe. The task of the pastor seems to be that of weaving the teaching materials of the Bible and the cherished memories of the ongoing Christian community of the church into the spiritual pilgrimages of individuals as they have to live and face life.

In brief, I have been bold enough to suggest both to myself

and to my reader that the point at which to begin in relating our use of the Bible adequately to the needs of growing personalities is in *the improvement of our own attitudes* toward people and the ways in which we habitually relate ourselves and our Bible to them. Until this is set right, nothing else will come right. Naturally, this is a continual process and goes on all the while we are doing other things to use the Bible in healthy ways and to develop healthy Biblical attitudes and ideas in our people.

Another rather obvious, but quite neglected, field of endeavor for the pastor can be stressed. The pastor himself should get into the actual process of the Biblical instruction of his flock from the earliest stages to the latest ones in personality growth. He needs an enduring personal relationship as a basis for all his work. He cannot do this task all by himself, nor should he wash his hands of the whole affair as a task not serious enough for his attention, as one that is such dull routine that he cannot be bothered. The sardonic grin that passes over many a pastor's face when " religious education " is mentioned is partly due to unhappy experiences in some seminaries, but largely due to our basic discomfort in the presence of little children and our inability to relate ourselves adequately to them.

The pastor, for instance, who sustains an enduring personal relationship to the children of his parish will covet the opportunity to participate personally in the vacation church school. He will communicate the Bible to children himself, bringing the rich store of all his years of study to the advantage of the little child and the teen-ager in such a way that he will not fear to hear their questions. They will learn from him to love the Bible by reason of the humanity, the simplicity, and the affectionate understanding of the man who first introduced them to it in church — their pastor.

In this particular respect the pastor of a small congregation has the advantage over the "busy" pastor of a large church. Likewise, the pastor who stays in one parish for most of his ministry has the advantage over the itinerant pastor. He can become fairly intimately acquainted with the children of his congregation and they become his guides in understanding the rest of his congregation. The pastor of a large church too often becomes alienated from the children of his church family by both his real and his imagined preoccupation. Quite often he becomes alienated from the children of whom he himself is the father. He delegates the function of teaching to others, and does not participate meaningfully *himself* in the experience of the children's learning of the Bible. The teaching of the Bible, more than most other types of teaching, is an experience in interpersonal relationships between the teacher and the pupil. This interpersonal relationship is the bond of communication that transmits spiritual insight and information. The pastor cannot effectively prevent damage from being done to growing lives in their contact with Biblical teaching until he has a healthy relationship to his people. But he cannot do so at all if he has no relationship at all!

In the study of the patients at Kentucky State Hospital that I have already mentioned, we were astounded to discover that in 51.5 per cent of the persons studied no influence of pastoral care in Biblical instruction was shown at all! And this was supposed to be in the so-called "Bible Belt" region. This was good in that harmful religious teachings did not complicate the problems of these people, but it is a rebuke to the pastors ministering near them, in that they were the men who were not on the job.

A third suggestion for the proper understanding of the most effective use of the Bible in the pastoral care of children and youth is dynamically related to the nature of a pastor's emotional frame of reference in his attitude toward the Bible and toward people. This suggestion is that the pastor needs enough flexibility and security both emotionally and intellectually to be able to stand having the Bible questioned. He needs to be more concerned with the anticipation, provocation, and acceptance of questions in children and youth than he is with the answers that he himself gives. Through his enduring relationship with many of them over long periods of time, he develops experience enough to *anticipate* the questions of youth and to provide help, both individually and in groups, on the questions that they have in common and tend most often to ask. Through his interpersonal relationship with them, and through the attention he pays to their parent-child relationships, he seeks to develop an atmosphere in which children and youth feel free to articulate their deepest questions. Such a spiritual communion will find enough examples contrary to its nature in the everyday life of the children and youth actually to provoke deeper questions in their minds. As Professor Tillich has said, " the church is a surrounding reality " that " shapes the existence of a child, and slowly transforms it," so that " truly eternal questions are asked."

Then the task of the pastor is twofold: both that he accept the questions with reverence for the personality of the asking child, and that he be more concerned with inspiring the confidence of the child to believe that he himself, with the pastor as a fellow seeker, is able to find the answer that meets *his* need. Paul Tillich calls this the discovery of the Bible as " the interior authorship of our own biography."

This is a very different procedure from that of " throwing answers at people's heads to questions that they never ask." It is based upon the conviction that even very small children suffer despair in the realm of hidden fears and confused loyalties, and in the response to these deeper realities children show an awareness of the infinite and an unspoken knowledge of the things that matter far beyond that of their elders. It is relevant at this point to ponder the saying of Jesus that " their angels always behold the face of my Father."

The pastor's work at this point is in vain unless he has the comradeship of the parents in his task. Therefore, he needs to pay exceedingly careful attention to the ways in which his suggestions about family worship in the home — its importance, its values, and its necessity — are being incorporated into the parents' treatment of their children.

Two illustrations clarify my meaning. A young woman said: " When I was in my middle teens, Dad decided we needed a family altar. (The family needed something to draw it together.) So he set a time (convenient to him) and sent out the order for us to attend. He forced the shoe on the foot without using the ' shoehorn of psychology.' The toes crumpled up. In six months the plan was discontinued, never to be fully resumed. You can guess what my attitude toward prayer and Father was! "

Another illustration is that of a father who insisted that all the children in his large family should participate in the reading of the Bible and in family prayers. One son rebelled one day, and said that he did not want to do so. The father told the son that as long as " he lived under the same roof with him " he would conform, particularly in family worship. When the son resisted even further, the father attempted to force him into a chair. The son balked and it turned into a fight with fists. The boy gave his father a severe beating and left the house, not to return until the time of the father's death several years later.

I have chosen these two situations to illustrate a vital factor in the transmission of Biblical truth in the home. The failure in communication arises more readily from disordered interpersonal relationships than from simple ignorance about the Bible. These are merely two examples as to how the instructions from a pastor concerning the family altar can be perverted by basic family and personality disorders in the home.

All the suggestions that have been made lead the pastor back to the point at which we began: his personal counseling contact with the families and individuals in his parish. Here the work of healing and the work of prevention are going on simultaneously, as the pastor seeks to fit the eternal message of the Bible to the transient, grimy, existential necessities of everyday living. In the last mentioned situation, the pastor does not appear anywhere on the " horizon of horror." If he had, he would have found himself seeking to understand not only the difficulties of the father, past fifty, or those of the son, in his late teens, but also the speechless terror of the silent, youngest daughter, age seven, who twenty years later told me of the agony that filled her life upon observing the whole scene! She said, " After the fight, we went on and had prayers anyway! "

I am simply suggesting in conclusion that the pastor both starts and finishes his use of the Bible in pastoral care of children in his intimate personal counseling situations. He equips himself with both the skill and the courage with which to discern what the basic questions and sufferings of his particular people are. He becomes saturated with *their* perception of things that are important. He feels *their* arrows by day and snares by night. He learns in particular what blockages hold them back from creative living. Through the interpersonal relationship, which is bound together by the Holy Spirit, the Bible speaks its message through the pastor at the level of every day's most quiet need, and becomes human nature's daily food.

CHAPTER IV

# THE USE OF THE BIBLE AS AN INTERPRETER'S GUIDEBOOK

THE most effective statement of the proper and positive therapeutic use of the Bible is stated in Rom. 15:4:

"For whatever was written in former days was written for our instruction, that by steadfastness and by the encouragement of the scriptures we might have hope."

The two roles into which the pastor is most often cast as a counselor are that of the teacher-interpreter and that of the comforter. A serious question has been raised by secular counselors, such as Carl Rogers and others, as to the relevance of either interpretation or reassurance to counseling. They almost taboo these two approaches. Their aim, to the contrary, seems to be to help their counselees to develop complete self-sufficiency and freedom from any need for a dependable authority. However, the older and more time-tested wisdom of the Bible, with a remarkable unanimity among its many authors, agrees upon the necessity for healthy dependence upon and fellowship with God as a prerequisite of true security and an open-eyed acceptance of the finite weaknesses and limitations of our human nature.

Therefore, the pastor who uses the Bible realistically in his counseling ministry cannot be dominated by secular concepts devised by men who have little or no knowledge of the Bible or concern for its place in culture and in the instruction, patience, and comfort of distressed people. When completely nondirective techniques are needed, he may either use them himself (if his time and relationship to the person permit him to do so) or he may refer the person to a clinical psychologist who uses such methods. We cannot necessarily call Biblical interpretation " counseling " in the narrow sense of the word. We cannot overlook the fact, however, that some questions about the Bible that are presented to the pastor are superficial and hide deeper and more serious disorders of the personality. That has already been illustrated profusely. But most of the questions asked a pastor are not of this order. They must be dealt with by means of sound instructional counseling procedures, which embody, nevertheless, permissiveness and person-centeredness. Here the pastor becomes concerned primarily with the tested and proved findings of modern counseling which aid him in being a better interpreter of the Bible. Here he will find the " attitudinal orientation " suggested by modern therapists extremely relevant, as he seeks to become a " person-centered " Biblical interpreter to individuals.

## SPECIFIC METHODS IN THE INSTRUCTIONAL USE OF THE BIBLE

The formal, or interpretive, use of the Bible in pastoral care calls for detailed attention. When a person comes and asks the pastor a direct question about what the Bible teaches, how can the pastor deal with the question without losing the values of person-centeredness and permissiveness in interpersonal relationships? First, the pastor should leisurely get acquainted with the person who presents a question about the Bible, and find out *why* he asked it. How did it occur to him? What need is he trying to fulfill? Or is it just idle curiosity such as: " Where did Cain get his wife?" This "hearing the person out" may take several interviews. I like to say to a person whom I do not know: "Before we can discover any satisfactory answer to your questions we need to become better acquainted. Tell me about yourself."

Such a suggestion is based upon the presupposition that every question that is seriously asked a pastor comes out of a subjective frame of reference composed of the successes and failures that individual has had in the "common ventures of life." The oval of interpersonal relationships to father, mother, brother, sister, fellow workers, and larger community encircles most of the questions that are asked us as pastors. If we do not have some "feelingful entree" into this context, we can no more adequately interpret the Scripture to that person than we do when we take a passage from its context and argue it from a "proof-text" position.

Again, the pastor should appeal to the counselee's own Biblical knowledge on the specific subject of his question. Notice Jesus as he asked in Mark 10:17-19:

"And as he was setting out on his journey, a man ran up and knelt before him, and asked him, 'Good Teacher, what must I do to inherit eternal life?' And Jesus said to him, 'Why do you call me good? No one is good but God alone. You know the commandments: "Do not kill, Do not commit adultery, Do not steal, Do not bear false witness, Do not defraud, Honor your father and mother."'"

Jesus was aware of this man's religious background, and the amount of knowledge he already had concerning the law. The pastor of today answers the question of a student in an engineering school in a very different way from that in which he answers the student of theology in a seminary who has had extensive Biblical training. The missionary on a foreign field has a very different problem in dealing with the questions of a

new convert from that confronted by a pastor of a church who
is answering the question of a teen-ager who has been in the
church school since his cradle roll days, and who has been born
into a culture that has had several generations of Christian
tradition.

Furthermore, on a subsequent interview, the pastor should
give the person a chance to reveal his *own* interpretations and
conclusions, encouraging him to raise questions for discussion
and exploration. The Socratic method of helping him to answer
his own questions is commendable at this point. It is more important that a person devise his own interpretation than it is
that the pastor press him into any prearranged or patent interpretation. As Paul Tillich suggests, there is a correlation between the questions and answers in such a situation. Every
question presupposes certain expected answers before ever it
can be formulated, per se. Both the pastor and the parishioner
participate in both the question and the answer. In the manner
of Jesus, we should always be at the business of shaping the existence of growing disciples in the direction of the questions
most often asked in the Bible: " Where are you? " " Am I my
brother's keeper? " " Who am I? " " Who is my neighbor? "
" What must I do to inherit eternal life? " " Who do men say
that I am? " When he comes forth from his own reflections, he
may have some instructive insight to offer the pastor, who
then finds his own interpretation enriched. This is the point
where client-centered counseling makes a creative contribution
to the pastor's role as an interpreter of the Bible. The spon-
taneous intelligence of a person in the press of a felt difficulty
quite often lays hold of a more realistic interpretation than does
the mind of the minister who does not feel that pressure so
keenly.

The pastor, also, should supply missing information concerning the passage of Scripture. Here we need to distinguish

clearly between *information* about the Scripture and *interpretations* of the Scripture. It is the distinction between empirically established facts and deductively or inductively derived interpretations of those facts. Here the pastor's specialized knowledge of the Bible comes into action. The knowledge of the historical process involved in the Biblical narratives, the technical difficulties of translation, the customs of Biblical times, the larger context of specific texts, and some of the personal biographies of the writers of the various books — all this knowledge comes to the particular aid of the counselee from his pastor if the pastor also is equipped with an equally careful knowledge of and concern for the personality of his parishioner.

The pastor's authority as an interpreter of the Bible arises not from his office as a minister, but from his having disciplined himself in the apprehension of factual knowledge concerning the Bible itself. Then his authority arises naturally from the amount and quality of factual information to which he has access, as John McNeill suggests:

" The scriptural theologians of today are helping us to discover anew the authority of the Bible as a guide to the will of God, the nature and the needs of man, and the availability of divine grace in daily living. . . . The authority of the psychiatrist is that of an expert in his growing science. That of the religious counselor must rest primarily upon his spiritual expertness " (*The History of the Cure of Souls,* p. 327. Harper & Brothers, 1951).

Many of the grossly pathological attitudes that become associated with the Bible could be avoided if pastors would take more seriously the responsibility of teaching the Bible themselves rather than depending entirely upon untrained teachers for this vital function. Frederick W. Robertson took his teaching ministry as seriously as he did his preaching. He lectured on Sunday afternoons to the people of Brighton and they came in great numbers and heard him gladly. The heart of his teaching was the interpretation of the Bible. This is the point at which the preventive ministry of the pastor and his ministry as a counselor converge.

Only after these procedures have been followed should the pastor's own suggestions and interpretations be made directly. Such interpretations should be immediately related to the problems the person has presented, the felt need he is trying to meet, and the life story he has revealed. They should be brief, to the point, and uncomplicated by abstractions. Even so, these should be *suggested* interpretations with which the person may disagree without feeling that he will lose the friendship of his pastor.

The pastor does not wish to be restricted to such formal uses of the Bible, however. He needs other more "saltlike" ways of pervading his interpersonal relationships with the insights and instructions of the Bible. Several suggestions have been tested in experience.

The pastor's own stream of speech, particularly in relation to people who love the Bible, should be filled with the literary smoothness and eloquence of the Bible. The use of Biblical language has long been characteristic of the literary geniuses of history. Today the pastor who is trained in counseling is prone to use psychological "jargon" in his speech. He often fails to communicate his real meaning with these relatively obscure and popularly misleading terms. The pastor would be more likely to be understood if he chose to stay in the Anglo-Saxon language of the English Bible. For instance, a more adequate word for "ambivalence" is "double-mindedness"; the most graphic expression of "projection" is the Biblical word "scapegoat." Further, the pastor who, by second nature, chooses the Biblical symbol is more likely to be thought of as a "shepherd" than as a "counselor."

Occasionally the pastor may carefully select the passages for consideration in connection with a given problem which his parishioner is facing. He can make an assignment for the person's own study of a specific set of teachings. Thus he lets the Holy Spirit have the first opportunity to interpret the Scripture. Many of the problems that people present to a pastor are rooted fundamentally in the relationships developed in their families, particularly to their mothers and fathers, brothers and sisters. And even in dealing with marital conflicts, careful attention to the roots of the difficulties reveals that they quite often stem from the relationships each marital partner brought with him psychologically and spiritually from his or her parental home. These relationships are not necessarily childhood experiences alone. The parents quite regularly are still living, treating their children in marriage the same way that they have always treated them, and their children's difficulties are present realities and not necessarily past memories that need resurrecting.

The Biblical teachings concerning the parent-child relationship have always been exceptionally healing as I have been able to call them to the attention of persons presenting the difficulties in interpersonal family living which I have described. They have the advantage of pointing to the real problem, giving instructive leads as to *what* the individual should do, and relieving him of unnecessary and morbid guilts that tend to appear when he begins putting these instructions into action.

Consequently, several recurrent problems in marriage and family counseling can be effectually relieved *at the right time and in the right interpersonal relationship* by the pastor who appropriately calls these teachings of the Bible to the attention of the counselee.

For instance, one may take the example of the overprotective parent and the overdependent child, both of whom come to the pastor, particularly with reference to the marriage of the child. One of the most difficult things a parent who is too emotionally dependent upon his or her children has to do is to " turn them loose " to their marital partners at maturity. One of the major causes of marital failure, according to Terman and others, is emotional immaturity in the contracting parties to the marriage. Jesus may have had something of this in mind when he quoted (Matt. 19:5) the Genesis interpretation of marriage (Gen. 2:24, 25):

" Therefore shall a man leave his father and his mother, and shall cleave unto his wife: and they shall be one flesh. And they were both naked, the man and his wife, and were not ashamed."

Whereas Jesus did not quote all of this passage, it is evident that he considered it valid as a standard for the interpersonal relationship of a person to his or her parents after marriage, and as an indication of the lack of shame with which a husband and wife should enter the oneness of their union.

Quite often, also, the pastor may have young persons coming to him expressing troubled spirits over the fact that their parents are opposed to their self-chosen and religiously motivated convictions as to what is right and wrong before God, or as to the type of work they should give themselves to under the conviction of God's leadership. Several instances need to be cited in order that this may be clear. For instance, a young college student, the son of a Georgia banker and plantation owner, feels called to be a missionary to Japan and feels that race prejudice, particularly toward Negroes in this country, is a form of injustice to be opposed. Again, a fourteen-year-old girl decides to be a Christian against the express opposition of her father, who prides himself on being an infidel. Or, again, a young mother sends for the doctor to care for her sick daughter. *Her* mother, the daughter's grandmother, interferes because she feels that her daughter should call a Christian Science practitioner.

Such persons, both parents and children, are quite likely to seek the guidance of pastors. Both parents and children are likely to quote different sides of the following paragraph of Scripture from Eph. 6:1–4:

" Children, obey your parents in the Lord, for this is right. ' Honor your father and mother ' (this is the first commandment with a promise), ' that it may be well with you and that you may live long on the earth.' Fathers, do not provoke your children to anger, but bring them up in the discipline and instruction of the Lord."

Furthermore, children who were neglected, even for some worthy cause which their parents were pursuing, have a way of coming to maturity in spite of the fact that they were neglected. Later, the parents become dependent, even as the children were earlier, and look to the children to care for them. One of the major social problems of today is that of the care of old people, persons who have no longer the strength to care for themselves. The care of elderly parents is one of the current problems that married persons present to the pastor. Too often they themselves have been so neglected by their parents that they have very little but social pressure and a sense of religious duty to motivate them to care for these aged parents. Jesus lays his finger upon the use of religious devotion as a rationalization for the neglect of elderly parents in his teaching in Mark 7:9–13:

" And he said to them, ' You have a fine way of rejecting the commandment of God, in order to keep your tradition! For Moses said, " Honor your father and your mother "; and, " He who speaks evil of father or mother, let him surely die"; but you say, " If a man tells his father or his mother, What you would have gained from me is Corban " (that is, given to God) — then you no longer permit him to do anything for his father or mother, thus making void the word of God through your tradition which you hand on. And many such things you do.' "

It is much more than incidental or accidental that Jesus interpreted the cross in the light of these teachings concerning the parent-child relationship. The crosses which people bear in quietness, those for which they seek no publicity, and from which they draw very little in the way of community support, understanding, or approval are the inner concerns they feel about their families. These are the wounds that draw no blood, but that keep many individuals in quiet desperation. For these reasons, and because of the fact that the bold truth of a teaching may be lost in the plethora of a commentator's words, I simply record *in a carefully chosen order* important words about the cross:

" Another of the disciples said to him, ' Lord, let me first go and bury my father.' But Jesus said to him, ' Follow me, and leave the dead to bury their own dead ' " (Matt. 8:21, 22).

" ' Do not think that I have come to bring peace on earth; I have not come to bring peace, but a sword. For I have come to set a man against his father, and a daughter against her mother, and a daughter-in-law against her mother-in-law; and a man's foes will be those of his own household. He who loves father or mother more than me is not worthy of me; and he who loves son or daughter more than me is not worthy of me; and he who does not take his cross and follow me is not worthy of me. He who finds his life will lose it, and he who loses his life for my sake will find it ' " (Matt. 10:34–39).

" One of the multitude said to him, ' Teacher, bid my brother divide the inheritance with me.' But he said to him, ' Man, who made me a judge or divider over you? ' And he said to them, ' Take heed, and beware of all covetousness; for a man's life does not consist in the abundance of his possessions.' And he told them a parable, saying, ' The land of a rich man brought forth plentifully; and he thought to himself, " What shall I do, for I have nowhere to store my crops? " And he said, " I will do this: I will pull down my barns, and build larger ones; and there I will store all my grain and my goods. And I will say to my soul, Soul, you have ample goods laid up for many years; take your ease, eat, drink, be merry." But God said to him, "Fool! This night your soul is required of you; and the things you have prepared, whose will they be?" So is he who lays up treasure for himself, and is not rich toward God'" (Luke 12:13-21).

"'I came to cast fire upon the earth; and would that it were already kindled! I have a baptism to be baptized with; and how I am constrained until it is accomplished! Do you think that I have come to give peace on earth? No, I tell you, but rather division; for henceforth in one house there will be five divided, three against two and two against three; they will be divided, father against son and son against father, mother against daughter and daughter against her mother, mother-in-law against her daughter-in-law and daughter-in-law against her mother-in-law'" (Luke 12:49-53).

"I have been crucified with Christ; it is no longer I who live, but Christ who lives in me; and the life I now live in the flesh I live by faith in the Son of God, who loved me and gave himself for me" (Gal. 2:20).

The use of Biblical figures of speech and symbols to clarify one's meaning often leaves an unforgettable interpretation in the mind of a counselee. For instance, a young theological student, who had moved from one stage of spiritual maturity to a higher one and was in turn suffering new conflicts and temptations, asked me, "Does one have to experience forgiveness through fresh repentance and insight daily?" After a long pause, I said, "You seem to want to know how the manna is gathered — once and for all, or daily with the dew."

Similarly, the counselees themselves often use Biblical figures of speech and symbols to incarnate their feelings. One person may say, "I have looked back at the town in which I grew up so much that I am afraid I will turn to a pillar of salt." Another person, feeling extremely guilty over his dependence upon his father, says: "No one who puts his hand to the plow and looks back is fit for the kingdom of God " (Luke 9:62).

Another more or less informal use of Biblical material is the use of proverbs and cryptic or dark sayings as a method of counsel in the hands of religious teachers. The proverb is a crystallized gem of racial experience which couches, somewhat obscurely, a profound truth. It has ordinarily been cut, recut, and polished until it can be easily remembered and pondered over from time to time. The Bible is replete with these sayings. They tend to be " dark sayings," with a hidden or cryptic meaning that " dawns " upon the hearer in an *unexpected* moment, usually *after* the teacher-counselor is gone. Examples of this may be taken from Jesus' ministry as he drew upon Hebrew wisdom: " Sufficient unto the day is the evil thereof " (Matt. 6:34, K. J. V.). "Leave the dead to bury their own dead " (Luke 9:60). " Render . . . to Caesar the things that are Caesar's, and to God the things that are God's " (Matt. 22:21).

These are what Aristotle called " lively sayings." They dart into the mind with the sharpness of a fishhook. They move into the memory like a fishhook, and can be removed only with great effort. An example from my own ministry is that of a young father whose wife had died in childbirth, leaving him alone with another child eight years of age. I was called to the hospital immediately to minister to him. I found him dazed, shocked, stunned. He was in no frame of mind for " much speaking." I sat with him in all the weight of his suffering, knowing that he was overwhelmed by what all this meant for the future. I said to him: " Let me help you to make the arrangements. Lean on all of us. But remember one thing from God's Word: ' Sufficient unto the day is the evil thereof.' " Months later he told me of his own accord that this saying had come to him again and again in his suffering, and had each time come in the light of new situations that arose.

The pastor who fills his memory with such proverbs of instruction as are listed below will find them therapeutically applicable many times in his counseling ministry. Used inappropriately they are like boomerangs that return, striking the pastor himself. Used with intuitive discernment, they are like arrows in the heart of the difficulties that rise up against a counselee's happiness.

" He that correcteth a scoffer getteth to himself reviling; And he that reproveth a wicked man getteth himself a blot. Reprove not a scoffer, lest he hate thee:
Reprove a wise man, and he will love thee.
Give instruction to a wise man, and he will be yet wiser:
Teach a righteous man, and he will increase in learning " (Prov. 9:7–9).

" The law of the wise is a fountain of life,
That one may depart from the snares of death " (Prov. 13:14).

" Better is a dinner of herbs, where love is,
Than a stalled ox and hatred therewith " (Prov. 15:17).

" He that is slow to anger is better than the mighty;
And he that ruleth his spirit, than he that taketh a city " (Prov. 16:32).

" Counsel in the heart of man is like deep water;
But a man of understanding will draw it out " (Prov. 20:5).

" The way of him that is laden with guilt is exceeding crooked;
But as for the pure, his work is right " (Prov. 21:8).

" He whose spirit is without restraint
Is like a city that is broken down and without walls " (Prov. 25:28).

" Answer not a fool according to his folly,
Lest thou also be like unto him " (Prov. 26:4).

" A man that flattereth his neighbor
Spreadeth a net for his steps " (Prov. 29:5).

" A fool uttereth all his anger;
But a wise man keepeth it back and stilleth it " (Prov. 29:11).

" Two things have I asked of thee;
Deny me them not before I die:
Remove far from me falsehood and lies;
Give me neither poverty nor riches;
Feed me with the food that is needful for me:
Lest I be full, and deny thee, and say, Who is the Lord?
Or lest I be poor, and steal,
And use profanely the name of my God " (Prov. 30:7–9).

" For everything there is a season, and a time for every purpose under heaven: a time to be born, and a time to die; a time to plant, and a time to pluck up that which is planted; a time to kill, and a time to heal; a time to break down, and a time to build up; a time to weep, and a time to laugh; a time to mourn, and a time to dance; a time to cast away stones, and a time to gather stones together; a time to embrace, and a time to refrain from embracing; a time to seek, and a time to lose; a time to keep, and a time to cast away; a time to rend, and a time to sew; a time to keep silence, and a time to speak; a time to love, and a time to hate; a time for war, and a time for peace. . . . He hath made everything beautiful in its time; also he hath set eternity in their heart, yet so that man cannot find out the work that God hath done from the beginning even to the end " (Eccl. 3:1–8; 11).

" Cast thy bread upon the waters; for thou shalt find it after many days " (Eccl. 11:1).

" The words of the wise are as goads; and as nails well fastened are the words of the masters of assemblies, which are given from one shepherd " (Eccl. 12:11).

" ' Those who are well have no need of a physician, but those who are sick: I came not to call the righteous, but sinners' " (Mark 2:17).

" 'The sabbath was made for man, not man for the sabbath; so the Son of man is lord even of the sabbath ' " (Mark 2:27, 28).

" 'Whoever does the will of God is my brother, and sister, and mother ' " (Mark 3:35).

The parable is the most used means of instruction whereby the Bible may be applied redemptively to the problems people present a pastor in a counseling situation. A clear example of this is found in the counseling ministry of Jesus:

" One of the multitude said to him, ' Teacher, bid my brother divide the inheritance with me.' But he said to him, ' Man, who made me a judge or divider over you? ' And he said to them, ' Take heed, and beware of all covetousness; for a man's life does not consist in the abundance of his possessions.' And he told them a parable, saying, ' The land of a rich man brought forth plentifully; and he thought to himself, " What shall I do, for I have nowhere to store my crops? " And he said, " I will do this: I will pull down my barns, and build larger ones; and there I will store all my grain and my goods. And I will say to my soul, Soul, you have ample goods laid up for many years; take your ease, eat, drink, be merry." But God said to him, " Fool! This night your soul is required of you; and the things you have prepared, whose will they be? " So is he who lays up treasure for himself, and is not rich toward God ' "(Luke 12:13–21).

It is easily discerned here that Jesus was faced in the first place with one of the thorniest of family counseling problems — the conflict of two brothers over the division of a family fortune — and he was pushed into the role of a judge in temporal affairs. In the second place, he refused the role of a judge, and redefined himself as a teacher by telling the unforgettable parable of the Rich Fool and his barns. Then he made the application in terms of a proverbial saying: " So is he who lays up treasures for himself, and is not rich toward God."

Of course a pastor is not and should not be restricted to Biblical parables. He should be able to create his own parables too. However, he has the advantage of the eternal elements in the immortal, unforgettable parables of the Bible. They should become the stuff of his thought, and he will find them useful in helping his counselees to cast the drama of their souls, to chart the pilgrimages of their long-range intentions.

Quite often the pastor finds his counselee either using a parable from the Bible or inventing one of his own. The pastor can use these vehicles of thought as means of communication and interpretation, falling into the lead that the counselee gives him. An example of a Biblical story used as a parable is recorded in my book, *The Christian Pastor:*

" Late one evening a minister received a call to come to a ward in the local hospital. Upon arrival he found an elderly farmer who had just been admitted. The man looked frightened and lonely, but a natural sense of humor welled up from beneath his anxiety. The minister introduced himself, and the patient said: ' I heard that you would come if I asked for you. It's mighty kind of you, because I need you. You have heard that story in the Bible about how some fellows was cutting wood one day and the ax flew off the handle and fell in the river. They had to call the man of God to help them get it out. Well, I sure have had the ax to fly off the handle with me. I never been sick a day in my life, and all of a sudden things went wrong and they told me that I have cancer of the colon. I got to be cut on Monday morning. The ax has come off the handle with me, and when the nurse told me that a man of God was close by, I sent straightway for you to help me get the ax out of the creek.' "

Or, again, the counselee may invent his own parable as one 42-year-old man did in the concluding interview of my series of six interviews with him:

" When I was a boy I lived in the country and was a member of a country church. We had a baptistry in the church, but no running water. For baptismal services we had to haul water in six barrels on a wagon from the creek. The water sloshed so on the rough wagon journey that by the time we got to the church, the water we had first put in the back barrel was exchanged around so much it was in the front barrel, and that water was in the back one. My life has been awful bumpy. What I thought was my job troubles was really my home troubles, and what I thought was my home failures was really my job failures."

Biblical characters afford another medium of communication between a pastor and his counselees. The use of the Biblical character appeals to the need of the counselee to identify himself with another more dramatic personality. For instance, this method was a favorite one in my work, along with a group of my graduate students, as chaplain of the Kentucky State Hospital. In my article, " The Diagnostic Use of the Bible " (*Pastoral Psychology,* December, 1950), which is included in Chapter I, an example of this may be found.

Real question has been raised by pastoral counselors and counselors who have no particular framework at all in which to do their work as to the relevance of any kind of interpretation in counseling. They do not restrict the idea of nondirective counseling to a more or less common-sense observance of the counselee's right to make his own decisions. They extend the idea to exclude any introjection of the counselee's understanding and interpretation of the particular issue under discussion, and conclude that this is the least desirable alternative to a laissez-faire relationship to the patient's thought processes as a whole. After quoting a record of an interview in which the counselor had given a very accurate interpretation of his counselee's problem, Carl Rogers, the main exponent of this view, suggests that " there is no doubt that the counselor's interpretation in this case is fundamentally correct. That does not make it any more acceptable to the student. . . . Interpretation, no matter how accurate, has value only to the extent that it is accepted and assimilated " (*Counseling and Psychotherapy,* pp. 26, 27. Houghton Mifflin Company, 1942). He might have added, as he does in another place, that the more accurate the interpretation is, the more likely it is to be rejected, particularly if the total life situation of the person is not " forcing his hand " to make a decision as to who he really is and what he is to do with his life.

Much of our interpretation of Scripture and our interpretation by means of Scripture of the problems people confront does run off the minds of both individuals and groups " like water off a duck's back." Nevertheless, Rogers' theory does not include the fact that a person has particular moments in time when he is more susceptible to an interpretation than at others. A person has " openings," as it were, when he can without fear accept and assimilate an interpretation at the core of his being and begin to act upon it. At such times the forces of resolve, as Heidigger calls them, tend to be a prepared seedbed at the moment of the fullness of time when the interpretation is planted. To overlook this fact is to ignore clinically demonstrable examples in our own personal lives, in our clinical experience, and in our knowedge particularly of Church history. The experience of Sigmund Freud who, upon having heard read one of Goethe's poems, resolved to become a medical doctor, is a case in point.

The matter of timing an interpretation becomes all-important to this point of view. After having revealed that: " He [God] has made everything beautiful in its time," the writer of Ecclesiastes says:

" For everything there is a season, and a time for every purpose under heaven: a time to be born, and a time to die; a time to plant, and a time to pluck up that which is planted; a time to kill, and a time to heal; a time to break down, and a time to build up; a time to weep, and a time to laugh; a time to mourn, and a time to dance; a time to cast away stones, and a time to gather stones together; a time to embrace, and a time to refrain from embracing; a time to seek, and a time to lose; a time to keep, and a time to cast away; a time to rend, and a time to sew; a time to keep silence, and a time to speak; a time to love, and a time to hate " (Eccl. 3:1-8).

In the timing of interpretation through the use of a particular Biblical thought, the pastor, as Carl Michalson says, " has discovered that he must have not simply the latest word or the ready word, but the *right* word. ' The difference between the right word and the almost right word,' to quote Mark Twain, ' is the difference between lightning and the lightning bug ' " (" Theology for Crucial Situations," p. 13, in *The Pastor,* March, 1952). This word does not usually come in the form of advice, but more by way of clear-cut interpretations that in themselves have motivating power. For instance, a pastor was listening to a businessman deacon justifying a particular business practice as ethical. The businessman said, " Well, a man has to live! " The pastor responded: " No. He doesn't have to live; the only thing he has to do is die." This was heard by an eight-year-old boy, who recalled it forty years later in times of decision.

Usually the openings of the mind that make a properly timed use of the Scripture appropriate come in the wake of the great crises in which the pastor is called into action by the appeal of the desperate person. The Biblical revelation has almost a startling relevance when the pastor (who has steeped his own mind in the thought forms and encompassed his spiritual perceptions in the redemptive design of the whole Bible) confronts the critical situation that occurs between him, a person in need, and the living God when he ministers to the needy person in his crucial hour. At such times the person has already seen for himself the insight that heals, and the pastor's use of the Bible becomes an aid to him in articulating and describing what he really feels.

The element of desperation enters into a person's sense of reality when he is thrust or thrusts himself into a crucial situation. It becomes an inescapable situation that requires decisiveness and presents a " live option " in which the person is suspended in a critical " either/or " position. This sort of situation creates " openings " of the spirit in which the pastor himself, even if he remains totally silent and nondirective, nevertheless is extremely participant and active in the determination of the person's perception of reality. For instance, a student was contemplating " leaving the ministry " because of the disintegration of his marriage. The forces of resolve were already in motion in this direction. He conferred with a counselor who was quite passive and did not participate intentionally or verbally in the student's flow of thought. On the second interview, the student said to the counselor, " I took from your silence that you felt that this is what I should do."

Nevertheless, at such openings of the spirit, the pastor should be exceptionally careful how he interprets the Bible (even if it is no more of an interpretation than the way in which he selects a particular passage) and what he says at such a time. The exigencies of the situation and the authority of the Bible, combined with the individual's need for the pastor's approval, may even combine to cause the person to take the pastor's advice!

Therefore, it is necessary that the pastor pay all the more earnest heed to his theological and Biblical understanding, and I quite agree with Michalson that " theology is no longer for the specialists alone . . . it is for the practitioners as well." At this point, the pastor's alternative is not restricted to a choice among Catholic authoritarianism, Protestant Biblical authoritarianism, or the theologically laissez-faire and indifferent counsel " which draws its insights from sources that have no necessary relation to the Christian faith." The alternative is that a pastor deepen rather than neglect his understanding of religious experience itself as it is related to the existential realities which the spiritual pilgrimages of all people have in common. He needs to develop (through astute observation and disciplined listening to his parishioners' individual complaints) an over-all understanding of the troubles that tend to be characteristic of their community and culture, and to know his parishioners personally so that his use of the Bible can be appropriate and well timed to their particular hours of need.

CHAPTER V

## THE BIBLE AS A BOOK OF COMFORT

D R. SPAFFORD ACKERLY, at the Silver Anniversary
of the Council for Clinical Training, said that one of
the purposes of religion from a psychological point of view is
to " create feeling tone," to stimulate and generate psychic
energy. The need for this type of creation within a personality
is illustrated by a person who came seeking the aid of John
Sutherland Bonnell. He said:

" My analyst has shown me that this nasty business had its beginnings when I was three years old, through the mistreatment of a
nursemaid . . . I know the whole story backward and forward,
but I am helpless in the grip of unwholesome desires " (J. S. Bonnell, *Psychology for Pastor and People,* pp. 30, 31. Harper &
Brothers, 1948).

Bonnell sensed in the man a need for the *creative* power of
faith. He used the Scripture: " I believe; help my unbelief,"
in a strongly suggestive and persuasive way as a means of
stimulating and generating the necessary psychic energy where-
with the man might accept responsibility for doing the thing
that he clearly saw was necessary and inevitable for his own
salvation and healing.

Bonnell interprets the man's situation in this way:

"I believe the insights he gained in the prolonged analysis were
a definite factor in his final recovery, but I am also convinced that

recovery would never have come about if it had not been for the upsurge of spiritual power within his life that turned defeat into victory " (*ibid.*, p. 32).

This is the unique element in Bonnell's use of the Scripture: He has laid hold of it as a therapeutic instrument by means of which he " puts heart into," or encourages, people. More closely discerned, this is the laying hold of new spiritual energies which hitherto have not been tapped in such a way that the soul of the person is able to move in the direction of its finite possibilities in God.

A minimum of research has been done on this " in-spiriting " ministry, except that which is classified in secular psychology as " supportive therapy." But the obvious examples of the strength imparted to helpless people through the use of the inspirational power of the Scriptures indicate that the so-called insight of the psychotherapeutic interview is cold and dead apart from some revelation of spiritual resources of creative power which are both deeper than the personal unconscious of the individual and higher than his personal conscious. This moves the pastor in the direction of a mystical interpretation of the interpersonal relationship between a pastor and a counselee. (Even an avowedly irreligious person is thrown back upon the facts discovered in the earlier days of psychoanalysis as to the persuasive and hypnotic effect of one personality upon another.)

Comfort is the second great purpose of the Bible prescribed by the apostle Paul in Rom. 15:4: " that by steadfastness and by the encouragement of the scriptures we might have hope." The ministry of hope-giving comfort is almost always necessary as the pastor becomes related to individuals who are going through the typical crises of life or who are having to adjust to inevitable life situations such as bereavement, chronic illness, or physical handicaps. Especially is the ministry of comfort indicated when the pastor is called upon to help to reclaim personalities that have grown bitter and hardened after a sharp disappointment such as a broken courtship or after a social and/or moral failure such as a divorce.

For instance, a 38-year-old woman came to me for pastoral help. She is the mother of a ten-year-old daughter and an eight-year-old son. She and her husband were divorced two months before she came to my office. She expressed her problem at the time of our interview in this way:

" My husband and I were divorced two months ago. I can't do the work I have to do for thinking about the way his mother and grandmother have wronged me by breaking up my home. I can't stop hating them. There's nothing I can do now, except just sit and think. I'm afraid I'm going crazy and will do something to myself."

I asked her to tell me the story of how she met, married, and divorced her husband. I listened to her pour out her sorrow as she talked with much tearful bitterness for an hour. She told me of having been to two other counselors, who, she said, " finally lost patience with me because I was not able to throw it off and go on about my business." (One was a pastor, one was a psychiatrist. I rather felt that she was projecting her own feelings about herself onto these persons, and that I might well expect her to begin soon to feel that *I* too had no patience with her.)

After having listened to her, I could see that she was still in acute bereavement over the loss — not of her husband — but of her security and status as a married woman. " There's nothing I can do now," seemed to summarize her whole situation of helpless powerlessness.

I pointed out to her that I would not try to give her false assurance by making her think that her burden was either easy or light. I agreed with her that there was nothing that could be done about the past — it was done. Yet, I pointed out that she did not have to bear the burden alone, because she had come to a man of God, who in helping her to bear her burden could fulfill the law of Christ, even though she would have to bear the great brunt of the load herself. Then I asked her to do three things:

1. To call me by telephone or come by for an office visit at any time when she became so discouraged and hopeless that she felt she desperately needed encouragement. My reasons for doing this were twofold: (a) In order to reduce her feelings of isolation and loneliness. (b) In order to help to ward off any rash or impulsive act in a moment of desperation and abject loss of hope.

2. To talk over any major decision with me *before* she decided to do anything that would change her living arrangements, work arrangements, or her plans for caring for her children. The reasons for this request were also twofold: (a) To give her some sense of dependence in decisions which she had not become accustomed to making alone. (b) To insure further that she would talk to me again *before* she should decide to do anything drastic that she might regret.

3. The third thing I did was to give her two copies of Paul's prayer in Eph. 3:14-21 (I have this prayer in printed form on a leaflet):

" For this reason I bow my knees before the Father, from whom every family in heaven and on earth is named, that according to the riches of his glory he may grant you to be strengthened with might through his Spirit in the inner man, and that Christ may dwell in your hearts through faith; that you, being rooted and grounded in love, may have power to comprehend with all the saints what is the breadth and length and height and depth, and to know the love of Christ which surpasses knowledge, that you may be filled with all the fullness of God.

"Now to him who by the power at work within us is able to do far more abundantly than all that we ask or think, to him be glory in the church and in Christ Jesus to all generations, for ever and ever. Amen."

I asked her to carry one copy in her purse and leave one at her bedside and to read it when things began to "feel too much for her." I asked her to think of that as *my* prayer for her before God. There were two reasons for this: (1) To develop a continuing fellowship of prayer with her, and gradually to encourage her to lay hold of the resources of God. I used this great Biblical prayer as a means of comfort. (2) To introduce, by means of her own private prayer life, a Third Presence in God, who will lower my personal importance to her. The presence of a third person, tends to direct and diffuse these feelings in such a way that the counselor does not become an indispensable emotional outlet. At the same time, the presence of God moors these feelings to their ground of being and goal of meaning.

This woman's problem cannot be solved by the easy twist of the wrist, but only by long-term, supportive encouragement and the emotional and spiritual transfusions that only the Christian "fellowship of suffering" can give. This type of ministry is what Russell Dicks has called "lending people your mind and soul." The feeling such persons usually get is that we do not, as pastoral counselors, have patience enough with them as they work through to their own ability "to withstand . . . and having done all, to stand." The "suffering with them" element of patience is too often professionalized out of the pastoral ministry because pastors become too busy to be bothered again and again by the same person, much less to set up a systematic plan whereby people are invited to bother their pastors for specific purpose and objective!

The Bible — its story of a cross to be borne — also holds

forth precious hopes both in and beyond the "present afflic-tions" of the moment. It is filled with comforting hope for cross-bearers, "from the burning of the noon-tide heat, and the burden of the day."

A few principles are obvious in the use of the Bible as a means of comfort and support in counseling:

*The pastor needs to be careful in his selection of appropriate passages as prescriptions.* Men like Bonnell, Dicks, and others who are most adept at this have a tremendous store of Biblical material at their command which they can use without clumsy reference to sources. The tendency of most pastors is to have a few, hastily chosen, unorganized bits of Scripture that they use indiscriminately for every occasion. The following passages are particularly useful in a ministry of comfort:

### I. THE FRUSTRATED

"The Lord is my shepherd; I shall not want.
  He maketh me to lie down in green pastures;
  He leadeth me beside still waters.
  He restoreth my soul:
  He guideth me in the paths of righteousness for his name's sake.
  Yea, though I walk through the valley of the shadow of death,
  I will fear no evil; for thou art with me;
  Thy rod and thy staff, they comfort me.
  Thou preparest a table before me in the presence of mine enemies:
  Thou hast anointed my head with oil;
  My cup runneth over.
  Surely goodness and loving-kindness shall follow me all the days
    of my life;
  And I shall dwell in the house of the Lord for ever" (Ps. 23).

This poem stands in the hearts of people as the pure expres-sion of the character of God as he is revealed in the needs of men. Closely related to it is Ps. 37:4:

" Delight thyself also in the Lord;
 And he will give thee the desires of thy heart."

These psalms are of particular comfort to a person who has
experienced the sudden frustration of a deep-seated and long-
cherished desire. For instance, the married couple who have
discovered that they can never have children or the parents
whose child was born dead are poignant examples. The pastor
also will think of other Scriptures he will want to use. It is a
very helpful procedure to have them printed without comment in quantity on separate sheets for " prescription-like " use
with persons who have particular difficulties. Sometimes it is
helpful to arrange Scripture portions into easily read lines, as
I have done in several passages in this book. The King James
Version may be reproduced freely, but modern copyrighted
versions should be reprinted only with permission. (See my devotional booklet, *Grace Sufficient*. The Broadman Press, 1951.)

## 2. The Disillusioned and Embittered

" Commit thy way unto the Lord;
 Trust also in him, and he will bring it to pass.
 And he will make thy righteousness to go forth as the light,
 And thy justice as the noonday.
 Rest in the Lord, and wait patiently for him " (Ps. 37:5-7).

" I had fainted, unless I had believed to see the goodness of the
  Lord
 In the land of the living.
 Wait for the Lord:
 Be strong, and let thy heart take courage;
 Yea, wait thou for the Lord " (Ps. 27:13, 14).

" ' And whenever you stand praying,
 Forgive, if you have anything against any one;
 So that your Father also who is in heaven may forgive you your
  trespasses ' " (Mark 11:25).

" Therefore lift your drooping hands and strengthen your weak
knees,
And make straight paths for your feet,
So that what is lame may not be put out of joint but rather be
healed.
Strive for peace with all men,
And for the consecration without which no one will see the Lord.
See to it that no one fail to obtain the grace of God;
That no ' root of bitterness ' spring up and cause trouble,
And by it the many become defiled " (Heb. 12:12–15).

After the person whose whole world has come tumbling in
because of miserable disillusionment has been permitted to
pour out the bitterness in a catharsis of negative feelings, the
pendulum tends to swing back and he or she begins to con-
struct more positive feelings and attitudes. This pouring out of
feelings needs to come quickly, lest they become rancid and
then turn chronic in bitterness. When the positive feelings
begin to emerge, the pastor may have already had these Scriptures typed on a card. He can hand this to the person for meditation. They may choose to read them together at that time.
Or, on the other hand, he may later send them on a card in an
envelope if he is sure that the person will accept them in a
spirit of understanding.

### 3. THE CONSCIENCE-STRICKEN AND SIN-SICK SOUL

" Come now, and let us reason together, saith the Lord:
Though your sins be as scarlet,
They shall be as white as snow;
Though they be red like crimson,
They shall be as wool " (Isa. 1:18).

And Jesus said:
" ' Come to me, all who labor and are heavy-laden,
And I will give you rest.
Take my yoke upon you, and learn from me;

For I am gentle and lowly in heart,
And you will find rest for your souls.
For my yoke is easy, and my burden is light ' " (Matt. 11:28–30).

" If we confess our sins,
He is faithful and just, and will forgive our sins
And cleanse us from all unrighteousness " (I John 1:9).

" For we have not a high priest
Who is unable to sympathize with our weaknesses,
But one who in every respect has been tempted as we are,
Yet without sinning.
Let us then with confidence draw near to the throne of grace,
That we may receive mercy and find grace to help in time of
need " (Heb. 4:15, 16).

" Likewise the Spirit helps us in our weakness;
For we do not know how to pray as we ought,
But the Spirit himself intercedes for us
With sighs too deep for words " (Rom. 8:26).

" By this we shall know that we are of the truth,
And reassure our hearts before him
Whenever our hearts condemn us;
For God is greater than our hearts,
And he knows everything " (I John 3:19, 20).

" And Jesus said,
' Neither do I condemn you; go, and do not sin again ' " (John
8:11).

" Jesus then said to the Jews who had believed in him,
' If you continue in my word, you are truly my disciples,
And you will know the truth,
And the truth will make you free ' " (John 8:31).

" See what love the Father has given us,
That we should be called children of God;
And so we are. . . .

It does not yet appear what we shall be,
But we know that when he appears we shall be like him,
For we shall see him as he is.
And every one who hopes in him
Purifies himself as he is pure " (I John 3:1–3).

The reality-based guilts of people concern them. When they begin to realize that they exist before God, and not merely before men, then their guilt thus becomes absolute and not merely relative, and they begin to seek forgiveness. They do not wish to be talked out of their guilt, or to be told that it is all right when they themselves know that it is not all right. Nor do they wish for some " psychological out " by which they can project the blame upon their heritage, or upon an unfortunate incident in childhood, or upon some irremediable bodily inferiority. They want forgiveness, and seek it in terms of a sense of being totally accepted by God, knowing that all human acceptance is partial and incomplete as compared with the acceptance of God.

The continuity of a counseling situation of this kind throws the pastor into a priestly role, and the things he hears as a priest he never repeats. This makes it impossible to give complete reports of such counseling. When a pastor has heard the person out, and the contrition is evident without being exhibitionistic or morbid, the use of the meditation of Scriptures, in the order that they are listed here, is invaluable. I have found them both healing and redemptive in their truth following the voluntary outpouring of feelings of sin on the part of counselees. The use of these assurances tends to lower my emotional importance to the person by increasing the importance of God through his Word.

## 4. THE FEAR-STRUCK

I use these terms to describe the person who is confronting a life situation that threatens in realistic proportion to the person's fear. I do not refer to the anxious person who tends in the direction of a neurotic way of life, whose fears are intra-psychically conditioned more than they are based upon external dangers. We learn from men under the severe conditions of battle that one of the causes of their emotional disturbances was the fact that they felt guilty over being afraid. In quiet desperation they were calling themselves names such as " coward " for being afraid, when they had every reason, biologically and psychologically, for being afraid. Usually in ministering to such people a pastor's first inclination when he turns to his Bible is to turn to the passages of Jesus' teaching that teach us not to be anxious about the things that will fill our lives with cares — treasures on earth that moth and rust can consume. The end result is that the person to whom we as pastors are ministering is likely to get the feeling that the Bible teaches that it is wrong to be afraid in the presence of real danger. His guilt, wrongly grounded, becomes a vexation to him, incapacitating him for any kind of action. This is the way fear paralyzes and allows the thing the person fears most to come to pass. As Hamlet said, in " fearing to be spilt," fear spilled itself.

We as human beings face a precarious existence and confront horror-producing dangers: the dangers of battle, the danger of serious surgery, the danger of untried and untested mechanical procedures, the dangers of life-risking occupations, and many people find their reservoir of courage constantly in need of replenishment.

I prefer in these instances to turn to the passages of the Scripture that refer to endurance, hope, and peace, because I feel that they more closely approximate in meaning what the

Anglo-Saxon mind means by "courage." Likewise, I do not turn to the passages that refer to fear, because to call attention to fear rather than its opponent emotions of love and courage is to strengthen its power. Furthermore, the sheer loneliness that fear produces is made more tolerable and fear itself lessened if the individual can feel as Jesus did and can say in the face of danger, "I am not alone, for the Father is with me."

> And Jesus said:
> "'But the Counselor, the Holy Spirit,
> Whom the Father will send in my name,
> He will teach you all things,
> And bring to your remembrance all that I have said to you.
> Peace I leave with you; my peace I give to you;
> Not as the world gives do I give to you.
> Let not your hearts be troubled,
> Neither let them be afraid'" (John 14:26, 27).

> "So we do not lose heart.
> Though our outer nature is wasting away,
> Our inner nature is being renewed every day.
> For this slight momentary affliction is preparing for us
> An eternal weight of glory beyond all comparison,
> Because we look not to the things that are seen
> But to the things that are unseen;
> For the things that are seen are transient,
> But the things that are unseen are eternal" (II Cor. 4:16–18).

> "For I am sure that neither death, nor life,
> Nor angels, nor principalities, nor things present, nor things
> to come,
> Nor powers, nor height, nor depth,
> Nor anything else in all creation,
> Will be able to separate us from the love of God
> In Christ Jesus our Lord" (Rom 8:38, 39).

> "The Lord is at hand. . . .
> In everything by prayer and supplication with thanksgiving

Let your requests be made known to God.
And the peace of God, which passes all understanding,
Will keep your hearts and your minds in Christ Jesus " (Phil.
    4:5–7).

" Through him you have confidence in God,
    Who raised him from the dead and gave him glory,
    So that your faith and hope are in God " (I Peter 1:21).

" Therefore, since we are surrounded by so great a cloud of
        witnesses,
    Let us also lay aside every weight,
    And sin which clings so closely,
    And let us run with perseverance the race that is set before us,
    Looking to Jesus the pioneer and perfecter of our faith,
    Who for the joy that was set before him
    Endured the cross, despising the shame,
    And is seated at the right hand
    Of the throne of God " (Heb. 12:1, 2).

" Therefore gird up your minds,
    Be sober, set your hope fully
    Upon the grace that is coming to you
    At the revelation of Jesus Christ " (I Peter 1:13).

Several other series of Scriptures could be organized by the
pastor according to the insight of his own experience in using
the Bible. Continuity of meaning is the key of the organiza-
tion, and the interpretation comes in the way in which the
pastor organizes the material and the subject which he gives it
to indicate the core of meaning that causes the passages to
cohere.

It would have been appropriate at this point to give material
for the ministry to the physically ill, the anxiety-ridden, and
the bereaved, but that work has already been done by persons
skilled in the ministry to each of these different types of pastoral care situations. Carl J. Scherzer, a hospital chaplain, has

prepared a volume entitled *Springs of Living Water* as a pastoral aid in dealing with the physically ill. Russell L. Dicks has spoken to the condition of the anxiety-ridden individual whose faith has been shaken. His volume entitled *My Faith Looks Up* will prove exceptionally useful. William F. Rogers has prepared a book that can be handed directly to the bereaved person also, which he entitled *Ye Shall Be Comforted*. All these volumes have made extensive use of the Bible in pastoral care situations to which they are directed. They are published by The Westminster Press in the Pastoral Aid Series. Other volumes for specific difficulties of people are in preparation and publication.

Not only should the selection of Scripture be done with precision, but another principle to be observed in the use of the Bible as a spiritual support to people is evident: The deliberate, suggestive, persuasive repetition of the passage or passages to the person in need is an important element in their effective use. The objective of this is to imbed the idea and thought of the passage just below the conscious level of the person's awareness in such a way that it will be unforgettable, and keep coming back like a song. The phenomenon of the snatch of a tune darting back into the consciousness without effort is analogous to the way in which the pastor should deliberately interject a Scripture into the thinking of the person.

Finally, the firm and positive conviction of a pastor as to the *truth* of the words that he quotes from the Bible as his assurance is indispensable. This is not loud assertion by tone or much speaking. This would most likely be felt as a pastor's protesting too much. Rather it is a calm persuasion that results in unquestioning and unswerving certainty: *Careful selection, effective reading,* and *vital belief,* then, are the three necessities in the use of the Bible as a book of comfort.

Naturally, the Bible can be misused as a book of comfort. It can be used as a sort of opiate to ease the pain of people who are really avoiding the responsibilities of mature life. It can be used as a means of keeping people on a sort of phenobarbital kind of religion that relaxes them into inactivity, but never commandeers their creative energies into a vital stewardship of life. It can be used as a crutch for people who do not need crutches, for they have long passed the time when they should be walking on the legs of faith that the Lord has given them rather than looking for some permanent crutch to carry them along.

The most dramatic instance of this that I have seen was that of a young mother who was becoming more and more seriously ill mentally every day. She had moved from a sort of panicky and undefined anxiety into fixed delusions of persecution and hallucinations of both an auditory and a visual nature. Her family and pastor recriminated her for her lack of faith and shamed her that her religion was not able to save her. They very much wanted her to be able to pray her way through the whole thing, without the aid of physicians.

I was asked to visit her and did so at her invitation. She revealed that she could not trust doctors to treat her, because she had been taught that we should depend entirely upon God to the exclusion of human aids in health. She said, " Does not the Bible teach that God will keep his heart in perfect peace, whose mind is stayed on him? " Knowing her overdependence upon her family, I said, " Yes, but it also teaches us that Jesus said: ' I did not come to bring peace . . . but to set a daughter at variance against her mother. . . .' " This was news to her and her husband!

The next morning her mother called me and I sought to persuade the mother to get adequate medical help for the daughter. Only with great difficulty could she talk about the matter, and I doubt if she ever permits her daughter to get medical help, so great is her domination of the girl. The comforting passages of Scripture are used as a tool in maintaining the domination.

After a pastor has come to grips with attitudes of this kind, he enters with sensitivity into the understanding of why it is necessary for a person in psychiatric treatment occasionally to depart from the use of his Bible for a season. It would be accurate to say that he should be encouraged to depart from its misuse permanently. The Bible was never intended to become such an occasion of stumbling to anyone, and we can appreciate the psychiatrist's position who would advise his patient to leave off reading the Bible until he was well. Nevertheless, we cannot condone the compulsiveness of some doctors who reject any use of the Bible by anybody at any time because of the patients that they have seen with pathological religious attitudes. Just because the patients come to the hospital feeling that the FBI is plotting against them does not present a doctor with a reason for crusading for the abolition of the FBI. Neither should it send him on a crusade against the Bible. Even penicillin has been administered improperly, and the pain-killing drugs become the scourge of the nation in the addiction made possible by unscupulous dope peddlers.

## Chapter VI

## THE BIBLE AS AN AID TO PRAYER

THE ministry of comfort is carried on in the hinterlands, at least, if not at the heart of the prayer relationship. Prayer is one of the inexhaustible sources upon which the pastor draws in his counseling ministry. He draws upon prayer for personal strength for himself as he bears other people's burdens with them. Otherwise, he would become spiritually poverty-stricken himself. He draws upon prayer as a resource to bring to the aid of those who come to him in any manner of affliction.

The Bible is an invaluable aid to prayer in the counseling situation, because it is predominantly a book of prayer itself. It is written in both the mood and the language of prayer. One of the problems a pastor faces in his counseling ministry is that of praying in trite and hackneyed phrases, of praying in the emotionally threadbare words of theology, or even of psychology. He feels the need for enriching his prayer thought with the great prayers of the Bible. In visitation and in counseling alike, the pastor will profit greatly in his own satisfaction with his ministry and most certainly he will redouble his usefulness to his parishioners if he will both mark these prayers in his own Bible and have several of them printed *without comment* on a card for use in his interpersonal relationships of prayer. I have recorded here my own paraphrases of several of the great prayers of the Bible. Some of them are printed verbatim.

" ' Our Father who art in heaven,
  Hallowed be thy name.
  Thy kingdom come,
  Thy will be done,
    On earth as it is in heaven.
  Give us this day our daily bread;
  And forgive us our debts,
    As we also have forgiven our debtors;
  And lead us not into temptation,
    But deliver us from evil ' " (Matt. 6:9–13).

### For a Discouraged Married Couple

Our Father, thou who art the God of steadfastness and encouragement, grant that these thy children may be enabled to live
in such harmony with one another, in accord with Jesus Christ,
that together they may with one voice glorify thee, the God and
Father of our Lord Jesus Christ. Amen (based upon Rom. 15:5, 6).

### For a Perplexed Doubter

Our Father, who art the God of Hope, fill this thy servant with
all joy and peace in believing, so that by the power of the Holy
Spirit he [she] may abound in hope. Amen (based upon Rom. 15:
13).

### In the Midst of Suffering

Blessed art thou, O God, thou who art the Father of our
Lord Jesus Christ, the Father of mercies and the God of all comfort. Comfort this thy servant in all his [her] affliction, so that
he [she] may be able to comfort those who are in any affliction,
with the comfort with which he himself [she herself] is comforted
by thee. Even as he [she] shares in Christ's sufferings, so through
Christ may he [she] share abundantly in comfort too. Amen
(based upon II Cor. 1:3–7).

### Upon Having Discovered a Way Through

Thanks be unto thee, O God, who in Christ dost always lead
us in triumph. We thank thee that through us thou hast chosen to
spread the knowledge of Christ. Amen (based upon II Cor. 2:14).

### A Benediction for a Person Going
### Into Military Service

O God, the Father of our Lord Jesus Christ, grant thy grace and peace to this thy servant. Grant that through our Lord Jesus Christ we may be delivered from the evils of the present age, even as thou hast given thyself for our personal sins, according to thy will, we pray. Amen (based upon Gal. 1:3–5).

### A Prayer of Comradeship with a Fellow Minister

We bless thee, O God, the Father of our Lord Jesus Christ.
We thank thee that thou hast blessed us in Christ
With every spiritual blessing in the heavenly places,
Even as thou didst choose us in him before the foundation of the world,
That we should be holy and blameless before him.
We thank thee that thou hast destined us in love
To be thy sons through Jesus Christ,
According to the purpose of thy will,
To the praise of thy glorious grace
Which thou hast freely bestowed on us in the Beloved.
For in him we have redemption through his blood,
The forgiveness of our trespasses,
According to the riches of thy grace which thou hast lavished upon us.
For thou hast made known to us in all wisdom and insight
The mystery of thy will,
According to thy purpose which thou didst set forth in Christ
As a plan for the fullness of time,
To unite all things in him, things in heaven and things on earth.
   Amen (based upon Eph. 1:3–10).

The following three prayers are general prayers taken from the letters of the apostle Paul. I have found them particularly useful in writing letters to persons with whom I have counseled as a pastoral counselor. They were originally written in letters to people about whom Paul felt very deeply. They are remarkable for the tenderness that they impart in a letter to one whom a pastor knows in the fellowship of shared suffering.

Furthermore, I have found that in those instances in which I find that a "bowed head" kind of prayer would be inappropriate, a pastor can turn in his Bible to these prayers and read them without the tension of a formal prayer. For instance, in a noisy hospital ward or hall, in a religious assembly crowd, or in any other confused situation where privacy is lacking and atmosphere for prayer is not sufficient, it quite regularly is an effective thing simply to look straight toward the person with whom you otherwise would pray and say: "As you think of me, I want you to know that I will be praying this for you. . . ." Then to make the prayer in a direct address to the person himself lends strength to the utterance. Naturally, the pastor depends upon his memory at this point.

### A Prayer of Thanksgiving

"I do not cease to give thanks for you, remembering you in my prayers,
That the God of our Lord Jesus Christ, the Father of glory,
May give you a spirit of wisdom and of revelation in the knowledge of him,
Having the eyes of your hearts enlightened,
That you may know
What is the hope to which he has called you,
What are the riches of his glorious inheritance in the saints,
And what is the immeasurable greatness of his power in us who believe,
According to the working of his great might
Which he accomplished in Christ when he raised him from the dead
And made him sit at his right hand in the heavenly places,
Far above all rule and authority and power and dominion,
And above every name that is named,
Not only in this age but also in that which is to come;
And he has put all things under his feet
And has made him the head over all things for the church,
Which is his body, the fullness of him who fills all in all" (Eph. 1:16–23).

### A Pastoral Petition

"For this reason I bow my knees before the Father,
From whom every family in heaven and on earth is named,
That according to the riches of his glory
He may grant you to be strengthened with might through his
  Spirit in the inner man,
And that Christ may dwell in your hearts through faith;
That you, being rooted and grounded in love,
May have power to comprehend with all the saints what is the
  breadth and length and height and depth,
And to know the love of Christ which surpasses knowledge,
That you may be filled with all the fullness of God.
Now to him who by the power at work within us
Is able to do far more abundantly than all that we ask or think,
To him be glory in the church
And in Christ Jesus to all generations, for ever and ever. Amen "
  (Eph. 3:14–21).

### A Combined Thanksgiving and Petition

"I thank my God in all my remembrance of you,
Always in every prayer of mine for you all making my prayer
  with joy,
Thankful for your partnership in the gospel
From the first day until now.
And I am sure that he who began a good work in you
Will bring it to completion at the day of Jesus Christ. . . .
For God is my witness,
How I yearn for you all with the affection of Christ Jesus.
And it is my prayer
That your love may abound more and more,
With knowledge and all discernment,
So that you may approve what is excellent,
And may be pure and blameless for the day of Christ,
Filled with the fruits of righteousness which come through
  Jesus Christ,
To the glory and praise of God " (Phil. 1:3–6, 8–11).

Naturally, Biblical prayers must, in many instances, be para-
phrased in such a way as to be made more personally appli-

cable to the situation in which a pastor is working. For instance, the pronouns can be changed so as to use the plural instead of the singular, or vice versa. Certain phrases that are not applicable can be left out.

The enrichment of the pastor's life through the dedicated use of these prayers enables a pastor to give form and beauty as well as power and meaning of utterance to his spoken prayers in a counseling situation, in pastoral visitation, and in pastoral correspondence, as well as in public worship.

The longer and more adequately a pastor functions, the more he will be called upon to carry on an extension of his pastoral relationships by mail. This was true of the apostle Paul, who might have written books that have been lost, but who wrote letters that are with us today. Our use of the lofty wisdom of the Bible, and especially of its great prayers, in our letters enriches them and gives them perpetuity. It is at this point that we most impart or most carefully conceal our warm hearts' deepest meanings. Whereas we do not want to become " Mr. Anthony " type pastors or " Dorothy Dix " type advisers to the lovelorn by mail, neither can we escape the use of letters to communicate with profoundly unhappy people. The Bible is a source of tested wisdom at this point; it can become a source of real insight and comfort, and most particularly of prayer, when used by a sensitive and considerate pastor in his letters.

## PRAYER AS A WAY OF INSIGHT

One of the basic values that has been re-emphasized by discoveries in the field of psychotherapy has been that of the indispensable nature of insight, or inner revelation, to the wholeness of personality. Prayer is often thought of as begging God for gifts or confessing to God that which we ourselves have already decided upon to be sin. These concepts of prayer, however valid they may be, tend to seal off its function as a means of insight or inner revelation. In the more legalistic frames of reference, prayer becomes almost a self-flagellation or self-exaltation experience. In the more liturgical frames of reference, prayer tends to become a set pattern that crowds out the creativity and spontaneity of the Holy Spirit within. Even in the use of Biblical prayers, this may become very true.

However, when we evaluate clearly the movements of the spirit in the prayers of the Bible, we see that the persons who prayed them expressed their truest and frankest feelings to God in prayer. In doing so they learned to understand these feelings themselves. For instance, we do not find any " squeamish nicety " in the prayers of the psalmist. We do not find the detached lack of inner communication of the Pharisee who stood praying. In fact, when we read the prayers of the psalms, we often wonder if the " Ipana-smile religion " of today would not have its halo dislocated by such a frank yen for inner reality of feeling! The authors of the Bible prayed knowing that they could not *add* to God's knowledge of them by revealing their darkest feelings to him! As they talked with him, they could say:

> " ' O Lord, thou hast searched me, and known me.
> Thou knowest my downsitting and mine uprising;
> Thou understandest my thought afar off.
> Thou searchest out my path and my lying down,
>     And art acquainted with all my ways.
> For there is not a word in my tongue,
>     But, lo, O Lord, thou knowest it altogether.
> Thou hast beset me behind and before,
>     And laid thy hand upon me.
> Such knowledge is too wonderful for me;
>     It is high, I cannot attain unto it.
> Whither shall I go from thy Spirit?
>     Or whither shall I flee from thy presence?

THE BIBLE AS AN AID TO PRAYER

If I ascend up into heaven, thou art there:
  If I make my bed in Sheol, behold, thou art there.
If I take the wings of the morning,
  And dwell in the uttermost parts of the sea;
Even there shall thy hand lead me,
  And thy right hand shall hold me.
If I say, Surely the darkness shall overwhelm me,
  And the light about me shall be night;
Even the darkness hideth not from thee,
  But the night shineth as the day:
  The darkness and the light are both alike to thee ' " (Ps.
  139:1–12).

Likewise, they were aware of the inner deceitfulness of the
human heart and the ways in which they could *attempt* to hide
things from God, but could succeed only in hiding them from
themselves. For instance, the psalmist says:

" ' If I had said, I will speak thus;
  Behold, I had dealt treacherously with the generation of thy
    children.
When I thought how I might know this,
  It was too painful for me;
Until I went into the sanctuary of God,
  And considered their latter end ' " (Ps. 73:15–17).

And in another place, we find this prayer:

" O God, thou art my God; earnestly will I seek thee:
  My soul thirsteth for thee, my flesh longeth for thee,
  In a dry and weary land, where no water is.
So have I looked upon thee in the sanctuary,
  To see thy power and thy glory.
Because thy lovingkindness is better than life,
  My lips shall praise thee.
So will I bless thee while I live:
  I will lift up my hands in thy name.
My soul shall be satisfied as with marrow and fatness;
  And my mouth shall praise thee with joyful lips;
When I remember thee upon my bed,

And meditate on thee in the night-watches.
For thou hast been my help,
　　And in the shadow of thy wings will I rejoice.
My soul followeth hard after thee:
　　Thy right hand upholdeth me " (Ps. 63:1–8).

Many of us in our more arid days of a religion without suffering and tragedy felt that the imprecatory psalms were low
forms of religion, and that such blunt expressions of hatred
and hostility as are found in these prayers should be " soft-
pedaled " in our teaching. Then we began to see the effects
that this refusal to accept and face hostility works upon personality. These effects came up in all forms of neurotic symptoms, and every manner of disease. One day they exploded,
geyser-fashion, and we, observing the plight of our counselees
and their families said, " We knew there was water there; but
where did all this force come from? "

But in Psalm 139 from which I have quoted above, a little
farther down in the passage, we find the words that follow,
which ordinarily we do not even like to admit are there:
" Surely thou wilt [or, O that thou wouldst] slay the wicked,
O God. . . . I hate them with perfect hatred: they are become mine enemies " (vs. 19, 22).

The regular ventilation, catharsis, bringing to light, and re-
sultant insight into one's negative or hostile feelings in one's
prayers puts them into their rightful context with the Eternal.
It lowers their importance along with the correction of our
self-concept, and it makes for better health.

With the modern loss of this kind of frankness in prayer
illustrated in the Bible, people have tended to look upon their
prayers as a means of communication between God and their
*ideal* selves, and not their *real* selves. Prayer as a means of access to the real self then loses its meaning. The only way the
darker self can speak is in profanity. One might say that pro-

fanity, as a habit, draws its psychic energy from the need to express one's deepest feelings. Profanity might be seen from this vantage point as a perversion of this need away from its rightful context in honest confrontation with God in prayer.

Particularly meaningful to parishioners is the privilege of honest expression in prayer when they are involved in acute frustration, incessant pain, and approaching death. The experienced pastor discerns early that childless couples, couples who have lost a child in childbirth, and husbands who have lost both their wife and a newborn child in childbirth have deep feelings of " complaint and provocation " toward God. As pastors (and particularly in our early ministry), we tend to feel the need to give " package reassurances " that amount to the platitudes that have been handed down to us from Job's advisers. We can sense the forthrightness of Hannah — her blazing complaint and provocation to God — and the mixed confusion but patient encouragement of Eli in the following " pastoral interview ":

" And it came to pass, as she continued praying before the Lord,
    That Eli marked her mouth.
Now Hannah, she spake in her heart; only her lips moved,
    but her voice was not heard:
    Therefore Eli thought she had been drunken.
And Eli said unto her, How long wilt thou be drunken?
    put away thy wine from thee.
And Hannah answered and said, No, my ʌord, I am a woman
    of a sorrowful spirit:
    I have drunk neither wine nor strong drink,
    but I poured out my soul before the Lord.
Count not thy handmaid for a wicked woman; for out of the
    abundance of my complaint and my provocation have I spoken
    hitherto.
Then Eli answered and said, Go in peace;
    and the God of Israel grant thy petition that thou hast asked
    of him " (I Sam. 1:12–17).

Pastors do well in these experiences with totally frustrated, "stymied" men and women to encourage them to pour out their souls before the Lord. The pastor can be a sort of third person in the "pouring out" in that the experience may not be a formal, "bowed head" prayer, but one in which the person expresses to the pastor as a sort of "umpire" the sense of injustice that he feels toward the Lord for the frustration he has to bear. The Heavenly Father can take it: the question is, Can the pastor stand to hear it?

Many pastors cannot take it. They cannot help dashing to the Lord's defense, even as did Job's counselors. They must arise to do battle with the sufferer in the name of the Lord. They become argumentative, talkative, and coercive. The modern Jobs say in different words but with much of the same meaning what Job did to his comforters:

> "'Lo, mine eye hath seen all this,
>   Mine ear hath heard and understood it.
> What ye know, the same do I know also:
>   I am not inferior unto you.
> Surely I would speak to the Almighty,
>   And I desire to reason with God.
> But ye are forgers of lies;
>   Ye are all physicians of no value.
> Oh that ye would altogether hold your peace!
>   And it would be your wisdom'" (Job 13:1–5).

Earlier he has anticipated his need to confront God alone when he says:

> "'For he is not a man, as I am, that I should answer him,
>   That we should come together in judgment.
> There is no umpire betwixt us,
>   That might lay his hand upon us both'" (Job 9:32, 33).

Chaplains in the years of combat service reveal to us that men in the presence of imminent death, bearing serious injuries, often tended to " carp at " and to question God. We find some understanding of them when we read the record of our blessed Lord himself as he asked why God had forsaken him. Earlier the importance of being able to stand hearing the Bible questioned was stressed. In hearing the groanings of the spirits of men in times of crises, the pastor cannot function adequately until he can hear without becoming panicky the cries of men against God.

He learns this, not by having read this book, or the books of other men, or even from having read the Bible. He learns it when he himself has faced the distillation of suffering, when he himself is able to say to God: " Out of the depths have *I* cried unto thee." Continuous exposure to the sufferings of others helps, but apart from the experience of having suffered oneself, it only hardens. Intensive clinical pastoral training aids tremendously, but it too can only professionalize unless one has himself been where he sees others struggling. When he himself has discovered that God accepts *his* real self, he no longer has to " defend God " against the real self of anyone else. The grace of God has been written in his "inward parts," and in his heart.

# CONCLUSION

WHEREAS I have sought to address these thoughts to the pastor who has not been technically trained as a pastoral counselor, at several points along the way I have intentionally raised problems that would be raised by the pastor who *has* had such training. I have a twofold objective for this: First, to stimulate the appetite of the average pastor to become more conversant with the problems of counseling and more participant in the task of counseling his people who come to him whether he is trained or not. Secondly, to deal directly with some of the easy generalizations made by professional counselors, which, if taken at face value, would tacitly tend to make the Bible irrelevant to the pastoral function of a minister, as well as to the needs of his parishioners.

The pastor who has read thus far will, I hope, feel as I feel upon having written thus far: that a more profound confrontation of the problems I have raised is in order. In the two appendixes of this book, therefore, I am suggesting two ways of confronting these problems more seriously.

In the first appendix, I give a bibliography indicating books now available in the various areas covered in this book in an introductory way, as well as a list of books in the field of pastoral care, pastoral counseling, personal guidance, psychotherapy, psychiatry, and psychoanalysis that are of primary value to a minister. The minister who feels that he cannot uproot himself from his pastoral duties can get indirect guidance through his reading program.

However, the best way is to enter into a program of further training in clinical pastoral work, either in a seminary that has resources for such training and/or on a less formal basis in institutional training programs in a hospital or delinquency school. In the second appendix, I list most of the resources for both types of training being offered in this country.

APPENDIX A

# A SUGGESTED BIBLIOGRAPHY
# FOR SUPPLEMENTAL READING

These books are presented in the order in which they should be read. They move from the simpler to the more complex, from the popular to the more technical, and from the purely pastoral to the purely scientific interpretations. Some of the books are of a frankly secular order, with purely secular presuppositions. But a pastor can no more avoid that which is secular today in any serious field of study than he can arbitrarily decide that he will not eat food that had been touched by anyone who does not happen to be a member of his denomination. Secular writers in this field often are used for higher and more religious purposes than they themselves care to announce from the housetops. If God is willing to let the tares grow with the wheat, we ought to have the courage and the willingness to work in the harvest. And even Jesus would not have us prevent those who heal, even though they do not do it in his name. If they are not against him, they are for him.

Careful note should be made of the fact that the following books are for the pastor's use in his study. Most of them were not written to be used as an aid to counseling by handing them to parishioners.

## PASTORAL CARE

1. Blackwood, A. W., *Pastoral Work*. The Westminster Press, 1945.
2. Dicks, Russell, *Pastoral Work and Personal Counseling*. The Macmillan Company, revised edition, 1949.
3. Oates, Wayne E., *The Christian Pastor*. The Westminster Press, 1951.

## Pastoral Counseling

4. Hiltner, Seward, *The Counselor in Counseling*. Abingdon-Cokesbury Press, 1952.
5. Hiltner, Seward, *Pastoral Counseling*. Abingdon-Cokesbury Press, 1949.
6. Wise, Carroll A., *Pastoral Counseling: Its Theory and Practice*. Harper & Brothers, 1951.

## Personal Guidance

7. Robinson, Francis P., *Principles and Procedures in Student Counseling*. Harper & Brothers, 1950.
8. Brayfield, Arthur H., *Readings in Modern Methods of Counseling*. Appleton-Century-Crofts, Inc., 1950.

## Client-centered Therapy

9. Porter, Elias H., *An Introduction to Therapeutic Counseling*. Houghton Mifflin Company, 1950.
10. Rogers, Carl R., *Client-centered Therapy*. Houghton Mifflin Company, 1951.

## Group Counseling

11. Carrier, Blanche, *Free to Grow*. Harper & Brothers, 1951.
12. Wittenberg, Rudolph M., *So You Want to Help People*. Association Press, 1947.
13. Wittenberg, Rudolph M., *The Art of Group Discipline*. Association Press, 1951.

## Psychiatry

14. Preston, George H., *Psychiatry for the Curious*. Farrar & Rinehart, Inc., 1940.
15. Preston, George H., *The Substance of Mental Health*. Rinehart & Co., Inc., 1943.

16. Menninger, Karl A., *The Human Mind*. Alfred A. Knopf, Inc., revised edition, 1949.
17. Hinsie, Leland E., *Understandable Psychiatry*. The Macmillan Company, 1948.


## PSYCHOANALYSIS

18. Healy, William; Bronner, A. F.; and Bowers, A. M., *The Structure and Meaning of Psychoanalysis*. Alfred A. Knopf, Inc., 1930.
19. Horney, Karen, *Our Inner Conflicts*. W. W. Norton & Company, Inc., 1945.
20. Freud, Sigmund, *Basic Writings*. Modern Library, Inc., 1938.
21. Fromm-Reichmann, Frieda, *Principles of Intensive Psychotherapy*. University of Chicago Press, 1951.


## THE PSYCHOLOGY OF RELIGIOUS EXPERIENCE

22. Rank, Otto, *Will Therapy; and, Truth and Reality*. Translated By Jessie Taft. Alfred A. Knopf, Inc., 1945.
23. Allport, Gordon W., *The Individual and His Religion; a Psychological Interpretation*. The Macmillan Company, 1950.
24. Kierkegaard, Søren A., *The Sickness Unto Death*. The Princeton University Press, 1946.
25. Buber, Martin, *I and Thou*. Translated by Ronald Gregor Smith. T. & T. Clark, Edinburgh, 1937.
26. Boisen, Anton T., *The Exploration of the Inner World*. Harper & Brothers, 1952.

## RESOURCES FOR TRAINING
## IN PASTORAL COUNSELING

### UNIVERSITIES

Boston University, in connection with the School of Theology, and under the direction of Professor Paul E. Johnson, offers work in the field of Psychology of Religion, which includes training in counseling, toward the Master's degree and the Ph.D. degree.

The University of Chicago, under the direction of Professor Seward Hiltner, and in co-operation with the Federated Theological Faculties of Chicago, has recently announced the offering of the Ph.D. degree in Pastoral Psychology.

The University of Southern California through its School of Religion, and under the guidance of Professor David D. Eitzen, offers the Ph.D. degree in the area of Pastoral Counseling.

### SEMINARIES AND DIVINITY SCHOOLS

1. These seminaries include in their curriculum some basic work for the B.D. and, in some cases the Th.M., which has two characteristics: (a) It is taught by professors who devote all or a major portion of their time to teaching in the field, which is variously listed as Pastoral Care, Pastoral Psychology, Pastoral Counseling, Pastoral Theology, and in some cases,

Psychology of Religion. (*b*) These professors have been trained in clinical situations under supervision, and have augmented this by specific experience in the field and with published research works.

Andover Newton Theological School, Newton Center, Massachusetts.

Drew Theological Seminary, Madison, New Jersey.

Duke Divinity School, Durham, North Carolina.

Garrett Biblical Institute, Evanston, Illinois.

Iliff School of Theology, Denver, Colorado.

Southern Baptist Theological Seminary, Louisville, Kentucky.

2. Other seminaries have part-time or visiting professors who teach one or more courses in their curriculum. Quite often these courses are taught by psychologists or psychiatrists who have no specific theological preparation. Others will have professors whose training and interests are absorbed in other fields, but who have counseling as a sort of " hobby," although they have no specific training. These courses of action are often prompted by the administrative problems of finances, understaffing, and the academic conservatism of the faculty in opposition to the functional diversification and liberalization of the curriculum. This academic conservatism does not imply theologial conservatism. Some seminaries offer nothing in the specific area of counseling, as yet.

### Extracurricular Opportunities for Training in Pastoral Counseling

Many seminaries have a direct relationship to agencies for training students in this field which operate independently of the seminary administration. The first two organizations in the following list are such independent agencies.

1. *The Council for Clinical Training, Inc.,* under the guidance of Rev. Frederick Kuether, 2 East 103d Street, New York 29, New York. The centers of training are located principally in hospitals and delinquency institutions in the Northeast and Midwest. The programs are twelve weeks in length. A detailed catalogue of their activities may be secured by writing to Rev. Mr. Kuether.

2. *The Institute for Pastoral Care,* with central headquarters at the Massachusetts General Hospital, Boston 14, Massachusetts, offers six-weeks programs of training. A folder of their activities is available for the asking also.

3. *The North Carolina Baptist Hospital,* Department of Religion, under the leadership of its three chaplains, and in cooperation with the faculty of the Bowman Gray School of Medicine, offers training the year round on every level of intensity and extensity. Brief seminars and lecture series, six-weeks programs for active pastors, ten-weeks programs for theological students, and six-months and one-year internships for prospective chaplains are offered. Information about this program may be secured by writing to Dr. Richard K. Young, Chaplain, North Carolina Baptist Hospital, Winston-Salem, North Carolina.

4. *Augustana Lutheran Hospital,* 411 Dickens Street, Chicago, Illinois, offers a short course for pastors under the supervision of Chaplain Granger Westberg. Information will be supplied by Pastor Westberg.